Lean
Italian Meatless
Meals

Lean Italian Meatless Meals

Anne Casale

FAWCETT COLUMBINE • NEW YORK

A Fawcett Columbine Book
Published by Ballantine Books

Copyright © 1995 by Anne Casale

All rights reserved under International and Pan-American Copyright
Conventions. Published in the United States by Ballantine Books, a
division of Random House, Inc., New York, and simultaneously
in Canada by Random House of Canada Limited, Toronto.

Casale, Anne.
Lean Italian meatless meals / Anne Casale.
p.   cm.
Includes index.
ISBN 0-449-98368-4
1. Vegetarian cookery.   2. Cookery, Italian.   I. Title.
TX837.C347   1995
641.5'636'0945—dc20   95-6099
CIP

Designed by Ann Gold

Manufactured in the United States of America
First Edition: September 1995

10   9   8   7   6   5   4   3   2   1

*To my mother, Rose Guarnieri Lovi, my culinary mentor,
who taught me the joy and art of cooking.
Her knowledge, wisdom, and guidance in the kitchen are responsible
for the heritage of health I proudly live and teach today.*

To you, Mamma, with love.

ACKNOWLEDGMENTS

Sincere thanks to my dear friend, David Wald, for his competent skills in reviewing the manuscript, giving suggestions, and helping me put my thoughts into words, and whose sense of humor kept me sane throughout the life of this project.

A big thank-you to my literary agents, Amy Berkower and Susan Ginsburg, for their support and encouragement.

My final thank-you goes to my husband, John, my official taste-tester. Thank you for your love, honesty, and after sampling and surviving eight variations of veggie burgers, never asking, "Where's the beef?!"

Contents

Polenta

Rice

Vegetable Entrées and Vegetable Side Dishes

Salads

Pizza and Focaccia

Desserts

Cookies

[BISCOTTI]

Introduction:
Lean Italian Meatless Meals

*P*ublic-health advocates are telling us to eat at least one meat-less meal a week to improve our quality of life. Campaigns have begun encouraging us to have a minimum of five serv-ings of fruits and vegetables each day. A diet low in fat and high in fiber and complex carbohydrates, we are informed, has been known to re-duce the risk of such health hazards as obesity, diabetes, stroke, heart disease, and many forms of cancer.

When faced with the idea of one or more meatless meals a week, many may panic. On the one hand, we can always turn to the meatless meals of our childhood: tuna-noodle casserole topped with crushed potato chips, baked macaroni and cheese, or any of those recipes laced with cans of cream of mushroom or cream of celery soup we made as beginning homemakers. Looking at these recipes today, they practically scream out: *High fat! High calories! High cholesterol! Stay away! Un-healthy!* On the other hand, we may find ourselves turning to vegetarian recipes. These creations, however, often call for unfamiliar, mystical-sounding ingredients that may not be readily available. When I wander into some health food emporiums, I feel as if I am in a foreign country. As I analyze some of these ingredients, they seem to be higher in fat and calories than I may care to risk.

I was not faced with this dilemma in taking the challenge of incor-porating meatless meals into my family's weekly menu planning. Some of my earliest recollections, in fact, are meatless memories. I can re-member, as a child, watching my mother prepare meals, and I always smelled something delicious cooking on the stove. I realize now that while the aroma was occasionally that of a tomato sauce with meat balls or a roast in the oven, more often what I remember were fragrant focaccia and pizzas baking in the oven, the scent of simmering thick soups and sauces, rapidly boiling varieties of pastas, bubbling risotto, or polenta—always combined with a variety of vegetables or legumes. Little did I know then that I was being offered a diet high in fiber and rich in complex carbohydrates. My mother, it seems, was way ahead of her time in planning healthy, meatless meals, not once but several times a week. Her use of fresh seasonal ingredients never sacrificed flavor or variety. While many people believe that pasta is the pillar of Italian cooking, Italians like my mother view vegetables as the foundation. She would cook at least two different seasonal vegetables along with the main meal for lunch or dinner. Those kinds of dishes are not only a part of my childhood, but also a part of Italian culinary history. Amazingly, they also represent today's focus on a healthy future.

In 1992 the U.S. Department of Agriculture released the Food Guide Pyramid, presenting the food groups with new emphases. At the base of the pyramid are the foods from which we should get most of our calories. The basic message of the pyramid is that we should cut down on fats and added sugars, as well as eat a variety of food from different groups. The chief eating goals, says the U.S. Department of Agriculture, should be variety, moderation, and balance. What you eat over a period of one week is more important than what you eat in a single meal. A diet primarily comprised of bread, cereal, rice, and pasta [6 to 11 servings per day], vegetables [3 to 5 servings per day], and fruits [2 to 4 servings], combined with low-fat protein sources [2 to 3 servings per day] and low-fat dairy products [2 to 3 servings per day] conforms to the Food Guide Pyramid, creating a well-balanced mix of proteins, carbohydrates, and fats.

The meatless recipes in this book are modified to deliver much less fat without sacrificing taste—even in traditionally high-fat, calorie-laden classics like Lasagne and Pizza. While there is not one recipe that exceeds 8 grams of fat, *Lean Italian Meatless Meals* is not a diet book. It is a collection of healthy, hearty, and delicious foods lovingly blended with childhood memories designed for today's improved life-style. Recipes are listed according to chapters: Soups, Pasta, Polenta, Rice, Vegetable Entrées, Vegetable Side Dishes, Salads, Pizza and Focaccia, Desserts, and Cookies. Each recipe includes a comprehensive nutritional analysis for calories, carbohydrates, cholesterol, fat, protein, and sodium. Read the

FOOD GUIDE PYRAMID

A GUIDE TO DAILY FOOD CHOICES

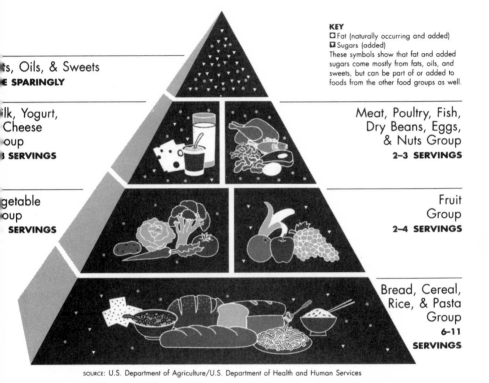

KEY
☐ Fat (naturally occurring and added)
▨ Sugars (added)
These symbols show that fat and added sugars come mostly from fats, oils, and sweets, but can be part of or added to foods from the other food groups as well.

ts, Oils, & Sweets
E SPARINGLY

ilk, Yogurt,
Cheese
oup
SERVINGS

Meat, Poultry, Fish,
Dry Beans, Eggs,
& Nuts Group
2–3 SERVINGS

getable
oup
SERVINGS

Fruit
Group
2–4 SERVINGS

Bread, Cereal,
Rice, & Pasta
Group
6–11
SERVINGS

SOURCE: U.S. Department of Agriculture/U.S. Department of Health and Human Services

the Food Guide Pyramid to help you eat better every . . . the Dietary Guidelines way. Start with plenty reads, Cereals, Rice, and Pasta; Vegetables; and s. Add two to three servings from the Milk group and to three servings from the Meat group.

Each of these food groups provides some, but not all, of the nutrients you need. No one food group is more important than another—for good health you need them all. Go easy on fats, oils, and sweets, the foods in the small tip of the Pyramid.

chapter on Nutrition Analysis if you are unfamiliar with the abbreviations used in these analyses. Exact measurements are given for each recipe so that you can achieve the same results that I did in trial testing. Make sure you read the headnotes over each recipe; they may provide tips on what to look for when shopping, possible ingredient substitutions, and suggestions for accompaniments to that particular dish.

The recipes have been adapted for you, the home cook, using contemporary ingredients in an easy-to-follow format. Most of the recipes are simple and can be prepared in less than one hour. Some are a little more complex. I have stayed away from purely trendy foods, preferring to select foods that are readily available in most supermarkets.

There is a revolution in the way we think about food. It is no longer enough that the end result tastes good. We now recognize the link between diet and good health, and healthy food preparation has become a challenge to us all. No doubt, some people will continue to scoff at the new cuisine of meatless meals. Here's how to handle them. Prepare a meal from this book, such as Veggie Burgers with Tomato-Thyme Sauce, Baked Rice with Ricotta, Grilled Portobello Mushrooms with Lemon Dressing, Mixed Green Salad with Fresh Tomato-Herb Dressing, Silky Chocolate Cream, along with a couple of Orange-Almond Biscotti, then invite them to dinner. Serve this menu proudly, with a smile, and without apologies or explanations. Experience the pride and satisfaction of sharing your personal commitment to good health and good taste with those you love.

Glossary: Ingredients

*L*ean *Italian Meatless Meals* is dedicated to anyone taking on today's multifaceted nutritional challenge: managing more meatless meals; striving for five or more fruit and vegetable servings per day; increasing our fiber and complex carbohydrates while reducing fats. To help you achieve the best possible results and to promote the healthier life-style we desire, I offer the following basic guidelines on ingredients.

BEANS: Beans have tremendous versatility in their use with dishes that include soups, pasta, polenta, rice, vegetable entrées, vegetable side dishes, salads, and pizzas. They are an excellent source of protein and iron. They are rich in vitamins, very low in fat, and contain no cholesterol. When combined with other complex carbohydrates, they provide a more complete protein than a steak, with only a fraction of the calories. In Italian cooking, favorite types include cannellini beans (white kidney beans), chick-peas, dried peas, lentils, and kidney beans. When a recipe calls for dried beans, purchase see-through packages in order to note the quality, condition, and color. When soaking is recommended before cooking, it not only helps prevent the skins from cracking or bursting while cooking, but helps return moisture to the beans, which reduces cooking time. This step also makes beans more digestible. I usually keep a supply of canned beans in my pantry for occasions when I don't have time to soak and cook the dried varieties. Be sure to rinse and drain the canned beans thoroughly before using to remove any additives that may affect the flavor in the recipe.

CHEESES: Italians love cheeses and have developed some of the world's most distinctive varieties. Limited amounts of the following different types of cheeses are used throughout the book for flavorings. To keep the fat content down, use the recommended amounts for each recipe.

- ASIAGO: A cheese made from pasteurized milk. It comes in three different forms: fresh, mellow, and aged. For recipes in this book, look for the word "mellow" on the package. For full flavor, grate just before using.
- GOAT CHEESE: A creamy mild cheese known as *Caprino* in Italian. Not only is it difficult to find, but usually comes packed in olive oil, thus increasing the fat content. For recipes in this book, I recommend Montrachet, which is available in all supermarkets.
- GORGONZOLA: This blue-veined cheese is made from pasteurized cow's milk and has a light, spicy flavor and buttery texture.
- MOZZARELLA: One of the most popular Italian cheeses. Rather than the whole milk variety, which is high in fat, small amounts of part-skimmed mozzarella are used for lasagne and pizzas.
- PARMIGIANO REGGIANO: This imported cheese from the region of Emilia-Romagna is made from whole and part-skimmed milk. The nutty flavoring of freshly grated imported Parmigiano Reggiano is matchless to any of the domestic packages or containers available in your local supermarkets labeled Parmesan. Purchase a small wedge at a time. To store, wrap in a thin layer of dampened paper towel and place in a plastic bag. For full flavor, grate just before using.
- PECORINO ROMANO: This imported cheese is made from sheep's milk. Its name is derived from *pecora*, the Italian word for sheep. Many of you will know it by the name Romano. Limited amounts of this nippy, sharp-flavored cheese from Rome are recommended for many of the soups, pasta, polenta, and rice recipes in this book.
- RICOTTA: Part-skimmed ricotta is recommended for the pasta, rice, and potato recipes that require baking. Do not substitute fat-free ricotta for these dishes. It does not hold up as well as the part-skimmed. Fat-free ricotta is only used for making Silky Chocolate Cream.
- RICOTTA SALATA: There are two different types; one is semisoft

and the other is matured to a dry, hard consistency. Both are pressed and salted ricotta cheeses made from sheep's milk. The one used in this book is the semisoft variety and must be grated on the coarse side of a grater.

COUSCOUS: These tiny dry pellets are made from 100 percent natural durum wheat (semolina). The quick cooking variety is used for recipes in this book. It is easy to prepare and makes the perfect accompaniment to a main dish in place of rice, pasta, or potatoes. Couscous is imported from the Middle East, France, and Italy and is available at most supermarkets, gourmet, and Italian specialty stores.

DRIED FRUITS: In addition to the always popular apricots, raisins, pears, and prunes, an ever increasing variety of new and unusual fruits is now available. Blueberries, cherries, and cranberries have now joined the ranks of the standard dried fruits. These new dried fruits have been incorporated in several biscotti recipes in this book.

EGGS: For baking, a combination of whole eggs and egg whites is recommended. When a binder is needed, fat-free egg substitutes are used. If you do not have egg substitutes on hand, use 2 whole large egg whites for each ¼ cup of egg substitute recommended.

FLOUR: Recipes for pizza, focaccia, and baked goods call for different varieties of flour. Read labels and recipes carefully. To measure, spoon the flour lightly into dry measuring cups; do not shake the cup, pack, or press the flour. Level lightly with the back of a knife or a narrow metal spatula.

- BREAD FLOUR: This type of flour is milled from hard wheat, which has a high gluten content. The high gluten in bread flour gives pizza dough a light, fluffy texture and also produces a more elastic dough, which makes shaping or rolling easier.
- UNBLEACHED ALL-PURPOSE FLOUR: An enriched flour made from hard and soft wheat flours. It is suitable for baking a complete range of products including focaccia, cakes, and cookies. If bread flour is unavailable, this type of flour is recommended for pizzas.
- CAKE FLOUR: An enriched bleached flour made from high-

quality soft wheat. This type of flour is used for making very tender crisp Anise-flavored Biscotti (page 199) and Mochaccino Biscotti (page 210). Be sure to purchase plain cake flour, not the type labeled "self-rising," which contains leavening and salt.

- WHOLE-WHEAT FLOUR: A nutritious and flavorful hard wheat flour made from the entire wheat kernel, including the shell, starch, and germ. When combined with unbleached all-purpose flour, it produces a very crispy crust especially good for focaccia.

NUTS: Italians love nuts and use them in many desserts, baked goods, and some savory dishes. Among the most popular are almonds, hazelnuts, pistachio, pignoli, and walnuts. Because of their high fat content, limited amounts have been used here for taste and texture. Shelled nuts should be placed in plastic bags and stored in the freezer because their oils easily turn rancid. After defrosting, place in a preheated 350° F. oven and toast lightly to bring out their full flavor.

OLIVES: Olive trees grow all over Italy, which explains the popularity of olives in Italian dishes. Different types of black olives are used in small amounts for their distinctive flavoring. The easiest way to pit olives is to place them on a cutting board and thump them with the broad side of a chef's knife. The pits pop right out!

- CALIFORNIA BLACK OLIVES are only used in making caponata. Do not substitute this type of olive in other recipes.
- CALAMATA, spelled with a *c* in Italian, are one and the same as kalamata olives from Greece. The succulent, mildly bitter flavoring of this olive makes it interchangeable with the gaeta olive.
- GAETA: These reddish purple olives, grown in the Campania region around Naples, also have a mildly bitter flavoring reminiscent of the Greek kalamata olives.
- OIL-CURED OLIVES: This type of imported olive is cured by mixing with coarse salt and leaving in the very hot sun for several weeks until shriveled. These olives should be thoroughly rinsed before using.

OLIVE OIL: Olive oil is the only fat used throughout the book. There are two different types of olive oil used. For recipes that simply specify olive oil, look for the word *pure* on the label and purchase the best quality you can afford. When extra virgin olive oil is listed, it is recommended for its fruity accent and enticing aroma, which come from the first pressing of the finest olives picked from different regions in Italy. It delivers a powerful olive color and distinctive flavoring for that particular dish, so a small amount goes a long way. In choosing either a pure or extra virgin olive oil, purchase small bottles at first, before deciding which you prefer. Your palate will tell you which flavor suits you best. When you find one or two you really like, stay with them. Throughout the book, directions are given using cooking spray to grease pans and broiling racks. This aerosol product is available as olive oil cooking spray. You can also purchase a spray bottle with a fine mist spray attachment at any hardware store. Simply pour in the pure olive oil and use this bottle for spraying. It is also excellent if you have steamed some vegetables and want to add a delicate mist of flavor. Whatever oil you use, whether it be pure or extra virgin, it still contains 14 grams of fat per tablespoon, so carefully measure the amount specified in each recipe.

ONION FAMILY: The different intensities found in the onion family, including garlic, leeks, red onions, scallions, shallots, white, and yellow onions offer a variety of tastes. Each type has a particular use and all share a starring role in the Italian kitchen.

- GARLIC: Fresh garlic should have very firm, tightly closed heads. The skin can be pure white or feature purple-colored tinges. Garlic is best stored out of the refrigerator, uncovered in a basket or bowl. For easy peeling, place a clove under the broad side of a chef's knife. Thump the blade to split the garlic's clinging skin; it will then slip off easily. It is better to chop or mince garlic with a knife than to mash through a press.
- LEEKS: Buy leeks with crisp, green, unwithered tops and clean white bottoms. Leeks should be straight and cylindrical. If the ends are very bulbous, the leeks will probably be tough and woody. Trim off a portion of the fibrous leafy tops before trimming the roots. Cut the stalks in half lengthwise and wash thoroughly under running water, holding the layers apart, until no sand remains.

- RED ONIONS: This type of onion is one of my favorites, probably because of my Tuscan background. It is relatively mild and tastes sweeter than the yellow variety.
- SCALLIONS: Select those with crisp, green, unwithered tops and clean white bottoms. Try to pick scallions with large, bulbous ends. Trim roots and any brown or limp tops before washing.
- SHALLOTS: These slender, pear-shaped bulbs are about the size of walnuts and are more perishable than onions. They should be stored in a cool, dark place. To use, divide the cloves. Cut off the tops and tails of the shallots. Peel with a small paring knife, pulling away the first layer of flesh with the skin that is usually firmly attached to it before chopping or mincing.
- WHITE AND YELLOW ONIONS: Yellow onions are considered to be the most pungent of all of the globe onions (whites are slightly less so). Look for ones with no trace of moisture at the base or the neck and with no growth of greenery at the top—a sign that they have begun to sprout.

PASTA: In purchasing pasta, select pasta made from hard durum wheat flour (semolina) without eggs. This type of pasta has a sturdy texture and a distinctive taste that combines well with both delicate and hearty sauces. I keep many different shapes and sizes of dried semolina pasta in my pantry during the late fall and winter months. During the summer months, I keep a limited amount on the shelves. Most supermarkets carry a wide variety of excellent pasta products. I recommend you sample the generic as well as the commercial brands until you find one you particularly like.

POLENTA: Polenta is produced by cooking cornmeal with broth, water, or milk. As the cornmeal cooks, it absorbs the cooking liquid and swells, thickening into a soft, golden mass. Polenta is stirred constantly during cooking, so it won't stick to the pot and won't produce lumps.

RICE: This grain is as popular as pasta throughout northern Italy. It is the main ingredient in the classic creamy risottos currently growing in popularity. Risotto requires a specific type of short, oval, pearly rice known as *arborio*. In other recipes, regular long-grain or brown rice may be used.

HERBS AND SPICES: Herbs are an essential ingredient in cooking true Italian dishes. For the past ten years, my daughters, Joanne and Amy, have planted my herb garden as a Mother's Day present. Herbs are easy to grow and hardy. Always snip your herbs from the plants with scissors. Gently wash the herbs in tepid water and pat dry before using. If you choose not to grow your own, look for fresh herbs in the produce section of your local supermarket. If they are unavailable, you can substitute dried herbs in many recipes. A general rule of thumb: One tablespoon of minced or chopped fresh herbs is equivalent to one teaspoon dried. When using the dried variety, rub the herb between your palms to bring out its full aroma and flavor. Dried herbs and spices should be purchased in glass jars and stored away from sunlight and heat. The following herbs and spices are used for recipes in this book:

- ANISE SEED: An annual herb grown mainly for its seeds. It has a spicy licorice taste. Some recipes call for crushed seeds to bring out the flavor. These can be coarsely ground in an electric mini-chop machine or crushed with the broad side of a chef's knife.

- BASIL: The most common basil of the more than 100 different varieties available is sweet basil. These whole bright green leaves are deliciously aromatic. Pluck off the tender leaves just before you use them, so they won't bruise or go limp. This is one herb that I prefer to use fresh rather than dried. It is available year-round at your local supermarket.

- BAY LEAF: Always buy whole leaves, never crumbled or powdered. Look for those that are still tinged with green; if they are more than a year old, they will have lost their flavor as well as their color; discard and purchase new ones.

- CHIVES: A delicate herb with a light onion or garlic taste. Chives can be grown in small pots on your window sill as well as in your herb garden. Once they come up, snip with scissors right to the base of the stems. This will keep them tender as they rapidly grow back. For best flavor, sprinkle on food just before serving.

- CINNAMON: Both whole stick and imported ground cinnamon should be kept on hand. The whole stick can be broken into small pieces and ground in an electric mini-chop machine or with a mortar and pestle.

- DILL: The pungent flavor of this herb is excellent either fresh or dried. If I purchase dried dill, I prefer the type labeled "dillweed."

* FENNEL SEEDS: These dried whole seeds have a slight licorice flavor, similar to anise. Some recipes call for crushed seeds to bring out their full flavor. Coarsely grind or crush the seeds as you would anise seeds.

* GINGER: Ginger comes from the root of the ginger plant. Peel the bark of the fresh root with a vegetable peeler before grating. Crystallized ginger is used in baking biscotti.

* MINT: There are many varieties of this herb. Peppermint and spearmint are best known and are usually labeled "mint" at your market. Most varieties are extremely easy to grow in an herb garden. My daughters usually plant this herb in large clay pots so that it does not take over my herb garden. To store fresh mint, place the sprigs in a 2-cup bowl or plastic container. Cover with 2 inches of water and place the uncovered container in the refrigerator. Change the water every 3 days and your mint will stay fresh for 8 to 10 days in the refrigerator. This is also a good way to restore fresh mint if it is purchased in the supermarket and looks a little limp when you get home. You can also store fresh rosemary, sage, tarragon, and thyme in the same manner. (I learned this tip about storing fresh herbs from my friend and colleague Arlene Ward.)

* NUTMEG: Select whole nutmegs and grate with a small grater whenever you need nutmeg. You will find the flavor much better than the powdered variety.

* OREGANO: Always use oregano sparingly because of the herb's strong spicy flavor. If purchasing the dried herb, look for varieties imported from Italy, Greece, or Mexico.

* PARSLEY: The flat-leaf variety, Italian parsley, is more pungent than curly-leaf parsley, and enhances the taste of innumerable dishes. To store, cut off about 2 inches of the stems, place in a wide-mouth glass, fill halfway with water, tent with a plastic bag, and place in refrigerator. Change the water every 3 days and the parsley will stay fresh up to 10 days.

* PEPPER: Pepper, both black and white, is probably the most widely used of all spices. The whole peppercorns are the dried

berries of the tropical pepper vine. The variety of black pepper I always purchase from gourmet shops is Tellicherry, which comes from India. White pepper is made from the same dried berries as the black, with the outer shell removed before drying.

- ROSEMARY: Here again, fresh is best. This is another herb that should be planted in a clay pot. I usually bring it into the house in early September before any signs of frost. I put it on my windowsill and I have fresh rosemary to snip all winter. Strip the leaves from the stems after washing. When rosemary is dried it has needlelike leaves and must be finely chopped with a chef's knife or with a mortar and pestle. Fresh rosemary is usually available in supermarkets and can be stored in the refrigerator in the same manner as fresh mint.

- SAGE: Sage has velvety, grayish green leaves with a slightly musky taste, and it must be used sparingly. This is a hardy perennial that is easy to grow in a sunny garden. Sage can be stored in the refrigerator in the same manner as fresh mint.

- TARRAGON: This herb is another with a slight hint of anise. The best variety to plant is French tarragon—it is not as easy to find in nurseries, but it has a wonderfully subtle flavor. Strip the leaves from the stems after washing. Tarragon can be stored in the refrigerator in the same manner as fresh mint.

- THYME: A hardy plant that is easy to grow. My daughters usually plant two varieties of thyme, French thyme, which has a more pungent taste, and lemon thyme, which has a faint citrus flavor. Lemon thyme is excellent snipped in a salad or over steamed green beans or zucchini. Joanne and Amy plant thyme in tall clay hexagonal drainpipes that are about 17 to 24 inches in diameter and at least 14 to 16 inches tall (available in lumber yards or hardware stores). These pipes are set at least 4 inches into the ground and then filled with topsoil. Once planted, thyme cascades over the clay pipes, making it much easier to snip. (If thyme is grown directly in the soil, the plants tend to creep and take over the entire herb garden.) Be sure to strip the leaves from the stems after washing. Thyme can be stored in the refrigerator in the same manner as fresh mint.

SALT: I recommend using coarse salt (Diamond brand kosher salt) for seasoning, because it is pure, contains no additives, and requires smaller amounts for flavoring. For baking, use common table salt.

TOMATOES: Pear-shaped tomatoes (plum tomatoes) are preferable in many of the recipes in this book because they have a firmer, meatier texture and less juice and seeds than the round variety. For blanching and peeling, see Technique for Blanching Tomatoes (page 126). If you use canned tomatoes for sauce, the best are the imported canned variety from San Marzano, grown in southern Italy. These tomatoes have a ripe, red, meaty texture. If these are unavailable, the canned plum variety from California are a good substitute.

SUN-DRIED TOMATOES: Today, sun-dried tomatoes have become more popular in this country than in Italy. Purchase in cellophane bags or in see-through plastic containers to make sure they are deep red in color. They should be reconstituted in hot water, and will deliver intense tomato flavor.

VINEGAR: Choose a red wine vinegar that has a clear deep red color. White wine vinegar should also look clear, not cloudy. Sample different types and you'll discover the brands you most enjoy. In addition to red and white vinegars, I keep balsamic vinegar on hand. This aromatic, concentrated vinegar is a specialty of Modena. Balsamic vinegar takes several years of aging to produce the best quality, so it is considerably more costly than ordinary vinegars. When you buy it, be sure the label confirms that it is balsamic vinegar of Modena.

Nutrition Information

$\mathcal{T}$he following information will help you to understand the nutrition analyses found in this book.

CALORIES (cal.)—a measure of energy in foods. It is recommended that you eat the number of calories that allow you to maintain "ideal body weight." Thus, appropriate daily caloric intake will vary from person to person.

CARBOHYDRATES (carb.) are found in foods as simple sugars and complex carbohydrates, and they are a source of energy for the body. It is recommended that complex carbohydrates from fruits, vegetables, grains, and legumes be increased in the diet, and that simple sugars be decreased. Complex carbohydrates contain fiber, which is beneficial. Carbohydrates contain 4 calories per gram.

CHOLESTEROL (chol.) is found in foods from animal sources—meat, poultry, seafood, eggs, and dairy products. It is wise to keep your daily intake to 250 to 300 mg.

FAT An excess of fat is thought to lead to many serious diseases. Current recommendations are to limit your intake of fat calories in a day (not in any one particular food) to 30 percent. To find out how many grams of fat you may safely eat in a day, multiply your total caloric intake by .3 and then divide by 9. For example, if you eat 1800 calories a day:

1800 (calories) $\times$ .3 = 540 (calories from fat)

540 (calories from fat) ÷ by 9 (calories in a gram of fat) = 60 (grams of fat, the total you can eat in a day).

PROTEIN (prot.) is known as the "building block" of the body. It is made up of amino acids and has 4 calories per gram. Protein is needed for growth, repair, and maintenance of cells, enzymes, and antibodies.

SODIUM (sod.) is found naturally in most foods. When eaten in excess, it can contribute to heart disease, high blood pressure, stroke, and kidney disease. Current recommendations limit a day's intake to 2400 mg. Salt is the most common contributor to high sodium levels. One teaspoon has about 2200 mg.

GRAM AND MILLIGRAM (gm and mg) are measures of weight. Nutrients eaten in large amounts, such as carbohydrates, protein, and fat, are reported in grams. Nutrients eaten in smaller amounts, such as sodium and cholesterol, are reported in milligrams. There are 1000 milligrams in 1 gram.

All analyses have been rounded to the nearest whole number. When the analysis is less than 1 gram, the actual percentage has been given.

—Lynne S. Hill, M.S., R.D.

Soups

Introduction

In an Italian meal, soup is always served as a first course or main course, but never served before a course of pasta, risotto, or polenta. Lighter soup recipes offered in this chapter, such as asparagus and leek, broccoli soup with garlic, chilled tomato-basil, or zucchini-rice, can serve as a satisfying lunch, or may be served as a first course before any of the vegetable entrées. Many of the heartier soups, such as barley, escarole, and chick-pea; lentil and brown rice; potato-garlic; and white bean and vegetable, can be served as a substantial main course when accompanied with hearty slices of Italian bread or focaccia, followed by a simple tossed salad. The one thing that they all have in common is that they are all wholesome, filling, nourishing, and extremely low in fat.

Broth-making is a ritual in any Italian kitchen and a significant element in lean Italian meatless cooking. Vegetable broth is the basis for soups, risottos, polenta, vegetable entrées, and braised dishes. It is incorporated in small amounts in many of the pasta, pizza, and focaccia recipes as well.

The foundation of any good soup is its broth. The light-bodied, flavorful vegetable broth recipe in this chapter will taste just like the ingredients you use, so be sure they're extremely fresh.

The following are a few helpful hints in making successful broth.

- Thoroughly wash all the vegetables before peeling or slicing. Several vegetables are cut on the diagonal to expose as much surface area as possible to bring out full flavor.
- You can substitute a large peeled and coarsely chopped Spanish onion for the leeks (unpeeled onion will make this broth bitter).
- The paper-thin skin is left on the garlic, but the clove(s) should be crushed with the broad side of a chef's knife for full flavor.
- The leeks (or onion), carrots, celery, and potatoes are simmered (or sweated) in 1 cup of water first; this breaks down their fiber to release more flavor. The rest of the ingredients are then added and simmered, partially covered, for an additional 2 hours. Remove from the heat, cover the pot, and let the broth rest for at least 1 hour so all the flavors meld together before straining, storing, or freezing.
- If you plan to use the broth within a week, it may be stored in plastic containers in the refrigerator. Vegetable broth can be kept in the freezer for 4 months.
- For freezing, transfer the broth to pint and quart plastic containers, leaving 1 1/2 inches of headspace to allow for expansion. Label carefully.

Broth can be frozen in ice cube trays for occasions when small amounts are needed for any of the recipes in this book. To do so, transfer 2½ cups broth to a 1-quart glass measuring cup with a spout. Carefully pour the broth into a 16-section plastic ice cube tray. Freeze overnight. Run the bottom of the tray briefly under warm water before popping. Transfer to plastic bags, seal tightly, and store in the freezer. Each cube is equivalent to 2 tablespoons broth. Broth can be frozen up to 4 months.

If you do not have the time to make broth, you may substitute low-sodium canned vegetable broth. There are many brands on the market today. My choice is the low-sodium, fat-free Pritikin brand of vegetable broth available at your local supermarket or health food store. I have found this brand to be the closest to homemade. You can also freeze any unused portion in ice cube trays for further recipes calling for small amounts.

To me, nothing is more homey or satisfying than the pervasive aroma that perfumes the house and fogs the windows the moment the soup begins to simmer on the stove. What I love most is the gratifying looks I receive after serving a hot, fragrant soup for family or guests. The feeling of satisfaction is fulfilled whenever there are requests for a second bowl.

Vegetable Broth

[Brodo di Legumi]

4 QUARTS

You can double this recipe if you have a 12-quart stock pot, but increase the cooking time to 2½ hours.

2 medium leeks (about 10 ounces), roots and tops trimmed, split in half lengthwise, thoroughly washed, and coarsely chopped

5 medium peeled carrots (about 9 ounces), trimmed and sliced diagonally into ½-inch pieces

5 large stalks of celery (12 ounces), bottoms and leaves trimmed, sliced diagonally into ½-inch pieces

2 large all-purpose potatoes (1 pound), peeled, quartered, and coarsely chopped

6 medium well-ripened round tomatoes (1½ pounds), halved, cored, quartered, and cut into 1-inch chunks

8 large crimini mushrooms (6 ounces), trimmed and thickly sliced diagonally

6 large unpeeled cloves garlic, crushed with the broad side of a chef's knife

12 sprigs Italian flat-leaf parsley

10 short sprigs fresh thyme or 1 tablespoon dried thyme

4 bay leaves

1 tablespoon whole black peppercorns

1. Place leeks, carrots, celery, and potatoes in an 8-quart pot. Add 1 cup of water and bring to a boil over medium-low heat. Simmer, uncovered, stirring frequently, until no liquid is left in bottom of pan, about 10 minutes.

2. Add all of the remaining ingredients and cover with 5 quarts of cold water. Bring to a boil over medium heat. Turn heat to low

and simmer, partially covered, for 2 hours. Remove from heat, cover pot, and let broth rest for 1 hour.

3. Strain broth through a fine mesh strainer into another pot, pressing on solids with the back of a large spoon as you strain. Discard remaining solids.

4. Cool broth to room temperature and pour into jars with tight-fitting lids. Broth can be kept in refrigerator for 1 week or can be frozen in plastic containers or ice cube trays for up to 4 months (see page 2–3 for storing method).

Per Serving: Cal. 27   Carb. 6 gm   Chol. 0 mg
              Fat .19 gm   Prot. 1 gm   Sod. 16 mg

Asparagus and Leek Soup

[Zuppa di Asparagi]

MAKES 9 CUPS, SERVES 6

When this soup is finished, the asparagus tips will still be tender, adding a nice contrast to the puréed mixture.

3   pounds medium-size asparagus
1   tablespoon olive oil
1   medium leek (about 5 ounces), root and top trimmed, split in half lengthwise, thoroughly washed, and thinly sliced to make 1½ cups

½   cup peeled chopped carrots
5   cups Vegetable Broth, preferably homemade (page 4), or low-sodium canned
½   teaspoon coarse salt
½   teaspoon freshly milled black pepper

1. Wash asparagus several times in cold water to get rid of sand. Using a sharp knife, cut off the woody ends at base of spears. With a vegetable peeler, peel stalks from the base of the spear up, leaving tips intact. Cut off tips and reserve. Slice stalks into ½-inch lengths.

2. Place the asparagus tips in a steamer set over 1 inch of water in bottom of 5-quart saucepan. Cook, covered, over medium heat until tender, about 5 minutes. Remove steamer and let asparagus cool to room temperature. Pour off 1 cup of cooking liquid from bottom of saucepan and reserve.

3. In a 5-quart saucepan, heat olive oil over low heat. Add leek and carrots and cook, stirring frequently, until vegetables are tender, about 5 minutes. Add asparagus stalks, reserved cooking liquid, and vegetable broth. Turn heat to high and bring to a boil. As soon as soup reaches a boil, turn heat to low and simmer, covered, until stalks are extremely soft, about 30 minutes (test by pressing a piece against side of pan with a fork). Season with salt and pepper and remove from heat. Let soup cool to room temperature. Ladle 2 cups at a time into food processor. Run machine nonstop until you have a smooth purée. Transfer soup to a clean pot; purée remaining soup. (Soup can be made up to 3 hours before serving.)

4. Reheat, covered, over low heat. Add asparagus tips and cook for another minute. Ladle into individual bowls and serve.

Per Serving: Cal. 80   Carb. 12 gm   Chol. 0 mg
               Fat 3 gm   Prot. 5 gm   Sod. 204 mg

Barley, Escarole, and Chick-Pea Soup

[Zuppa alla Lorena]

MAKES 12 CUPS, SERVES 8

This is an adaptation of an old family recipe I received from my cousin, Lorraine Lovi Mullen. If you like, substitute red kidney or white cannellini beans for the chick-peas.

1 medium head escarole (about 1¼ pounds)	technique), and coarsely chopped with juice included
1½ tablespoons olive oil	
½ cup chopped red onion	½ cup medium pearl barley
½ cup peeled diced parsnips	1 tablespoon minced fresh sage or 1 teaspoon crumbled dried sage
½ cup peeled diced carrots	
2½ quarts Vegetable Broth, preferably homemade (page 4), or low-sodium canned	1 can chick-peas (16 ounces), rinsed and well drained
2 teaspoons minced garlic	1 teaspoon coarse salt
4 medium plum tomatoes, (about 8 ounces), blanched, peeled (see page 126 for	½ teaspoon freshly milled black pepper
	8 teaspoons freshly grated imported Parmesan cheese

1. Trim off and discard any wilted or bruised leaves from escarole. Separate leaves and trim off about 1 inch of tough bottom ends. Wash several times in tepid water to get rid of grit. If leaves are more than 3 inches wide, slice each in half lengthwise and then crosswise into ½-inch lengths; set aside.
2. In a heavy 5-quart saucepan, heat olive oil over low heat. Add onion, parsnips, and carrots; cook, stirring frequently, until vegeta-

bles are soft, about 5 minutes. (If vegetables start to stick to bottom of pan, stir in 2 tablespoons vegetable broth to loosen.) Stir in garlic and tomatoes; cook for an additional 5 minutes. Add broth and bring to a boil over medium heat. As soon as soup reaches a boil, stir in barley. Turn heat to low and cook, covered, stirring once or twice, until barley is tender, about 45 minutes. Stir in escarole and sage, cover pan, and continue to simmer until escarole is tender, about 15 to 20 minutes. Stir in chick-peas and cook for an additional 5 minutes. Season with salt and pepper; remove from heat. Ladle into bowls, sprinkle each serving with 1 teaspoon Parmesan cheese, and serve.

Per Serving: Cal. 177   Carb. 30 gm   Chol. 1 mg
              Fat 4 gm   Prot. 6 gm   Sod. 207 mg

Broccoli Soup with Garlic

[Zuppa di Broccoli con Aglio]

❖

MAKES 7½ CUPS, SERVES 4

This soup is quick to assemble and ready to serve in less than an hour. If you like, place a slice of toasted Italian bread in the bottom of each soup plate before pouring this old-fashioned homey family soup over top. It is also good with a little Parmesan cheese sprinkled on top.

1	large bunch broccoli (about 1½ pounds)		preferably homemade (page 4), or low-sodium canned
2	teaspoons olive oil		
4	medium cloves garlic, peeled and sliced paper-thin	1½	teaspoons minced fresh thyme or ½ teaspoon dried thyme
⅓	cup finely chopped parsnip, peeled before chopping	¼	teaspoon coarse salt
3½	cups Vegetable Broth,	¼	teaspoon freshly milled black pepper

1. Remove florets from broccoli, leaving about ½ inch of floret stems. Cut florets into ½-inch pieces; wash in cold water, drain, and set aside. Remove and discard the large coarse leaves from stems; cut off about 1 inch of tough lower part. Wash and peel stems with vegetable peeler; chop fine.

2. In a heavy 5-quart saucepan, heat olive oil over low heat. Add garlic and parsnip and sauté, stirring frequently until tender-crisp, about 2 minutes. (If vegetables start to stick to bottom of pan, loosen with 2 tablespoons of broth to prevent scorching). Stir in broccoli stems, broth, and thyme. Turn heat to high and bring to a boil. As soon as soup reaches a boil, turn heat to low and simmer, partially covered, for 35 minutes. Stir in broccoli florets and cook

until very tender, about 10 minutes. Season with salt and pepper. Remove from heat, ladle into individual bowls, and serve.

Per Serving: Cal. 89   Carb. 14 gm   Chol. 0 mg
              Fat 3 gm   Prot. 4 gm   Sod. 137 mg

Chilled Tomato-Basil Soup

[Zuppa Fredda di Pomodoro]

MAKES 7 CUPS, SERVES 6

A light refreshing soup to serve as a first course during the hot summer months, this soup may be made up to 2 days before serving.

6   large well-ripened round tomatoes (about 3 pounds), blanched and peeled (see page 126 for technique), cut into 1-inch chunks, with juice reserved
¼   cup fresh basil leaves
1   tablespoon plus 1 teaspoon cornstarch
1   cup Vegetable Broth, preferably homemade

(page 4), or low-sodium canned
1   tablespoon strained fresh lemon juice
1   teaspoon sugar
½   teaspoon coarse salt
½   teaspoon freshly milled white pepper
2   tablespoons snipped fresh chives, for garnish

1. Place half of the tomatoes and 2 tablespoons basil in food processor; process until basil is finely minced and tomatoes are puréed, about 1 minute. Transfer to 4-quart saucepan. Repeat with remaining tomatoes and basil. Pour in reserved juice and stir to combine.

2. In a small bowl, whisk the cornstarch into broth until completely dissolved; stir into tomato mixture.
3. Bring the mixture to a boil, stirring constantly, over medium heat. As soon as it comes to a boil, turn heat to low and cook, stirring frequently, for 5 minutes. Remove from heat and stir in lemon juice, sugar, salt, and pepper. Cover pot and cool to room temperature. Transfer to deep bowl, cover with plastic wrap, and place in refrigerator for at least 4 hours or overnight.
4. When ready to serve, ladle chilled soup into individual bowls, preferably glass, and garnish each with 1 teaspoon snipped chives.

Per Serving: Cal. 60   Carb. 14 gm   Chol. 0 mg
             Fat .73 gm   Prot. 2 gm   Sod. 144 mg

Potato-Garlic Soup

[Zuppa di Patate ed Aglio]

MAKES 9 CUPS, SERVES 6

A velvety smooth soup for anyone who loves the flavor of garlic.

1	tablespoon olive oil	2	quarts water
3½	tablespoons minced garlic	½	teaspoon coarse salt
½	cup finely chopped celery, strings removed before chopping	½	teaspoon freshly milled white pepper
2	large baking potatoes (about 1½ pounds), peeled and cut into ½-inch dice	¼	cup minced Italian flat-leaf parsley

1. In a heavy 5-quart saucepan, heat olive oil over low heat. Add garlic, celery, and potatoes. Cook, stirring frequently, until the vegetables are a pale golden color, about 6 minutes. If vegetables start to stick to bottom of pan, loosen with ¼ cup water. Add remaining water and bring to a boil over medium-high heat. As soon as soup reaches a boil, turn heat to low and simmer, covered, stirring frequently, until the potatoes and celery are extremely soft, about 25 minutes. Season with salt and pepper; remove from heat. Let soup cool to room temperature. Ladle 2 cups into food processor. Run machine nonstop until you have a smooth purée. Transfer soup to a clean pot; purée remaining soup. (Soup can be prepared up to 2 hours before serving.)

2. Reheat soup, covered, stirring frequently, over low heat. Stir in minced parsley and remove from heat. Ladle into individual bowls and serve.

Per Serving: Cal. 99   Carb. 18 gm   Chol. 0 mg
                     Fat 2 gm   Prot. 2 gm   Sod. 138 mg

Herbed Split Pea Soup

[Zuppa di Piselli ed Erbe]

MAKES 10 CUPS, SERVES 8

This is a somewhat modern rendition of an old-fashioned, rustic soup my mother made at least once a month during late fall and early winter. For a more elegant soup, cool to room temperature, ladle 3 cups of soup at a time into food processor, and process until you have a creamy purée. Reheat and garnish as suggested.

1 tablespoon olive oil
½ cup finely chopped shallots
1 pound dried green split peas, picked over to remove any foreign matter, rinsed, and drained
½ cup peeled diced carrots
½ cup peeled diced parsnips
½ cup diced celery, strings removed before dicing
2 large bay leaves
1 tablespoon minced fresh thyme or 1 teaspoon dried thyme
2 quarts Vegetable Broth, preferably homemade (page 4), or low-sodium canned
½ teaspoon coarse salt
½ teaspoon freshly milled black pepper
8 teaspoons minced fresh mint, for garnish

In a heavy 5-quart pot, heat olive oil over low heat. Add shallots and cook, stirring frequently, until lightly golden, about 5 minutes. Add the split peas, carrots, parsnips, celery, bay leaves, thyme, and broth. Cover pot and bring to a boil over medium heat. As soon as liquid reaches a boil, turn heat to low and simmer, partially covered, stirring frequently, until split peas are tender, about 1 hour. Season with salt and pepper and remove from heat. (Soup can be made up to 3 hours before serving. It will thicken as it stands. If you like, it may be thinned with ½ to 1 cup water.) Discard bay leaves. Reheat soup over low heat. Ladle into individual bowls, garnish each with 1 teaspoon minced fresh mint, and serve.

Per Serving: Cal. 255 Carb. 45 gm Chol. 0 mg
             Fat 3 gm   Prot. 15 gm Sod. 127 mg

〰〰〰〰〰〰〰〰〰〰〰〰〰〰〰〰〰〰〰〰〰〰〰〰〰〰〰〰〰〰〰〰〰〰〰〰

Lentil and Brown Rice Soup

[Zuppa di Lenticchie e Riso]

❖

MAKES 12 CUPS, SERVES 8

Simmering the leeks, carrots, and celery in a little broth first will release a more intense flavor to the soup than would simply boiling the whole mixture together. To round off this hearty one-dish meal, serve with Baby Spinach, Walnut, and Goat Cheese Salad (page 147) and some crusty Italian bread.

1 medium leek (about 5 ounces), root and top trimmed, split in half lengthwise, thoroughly washed, and thinly sliced to make 1½ cups

1 cup peeled diced carrots

½ cup diced celery, strings removed before dicing

2 quarts Vegetable Broth, preferably homemade (page 4), or low-sodium canned

2 cups water

½ cup brown rice, picked over to remove any dark brown grains

2 cups lentils, picked over to remove any foreign matter, rinsed, and drained

8 medium, well-ripened plum tomatoes (about 1 pound), blanched and peeled (see page 126 for technique), coarsely chopped, with juice included

1 tablespoon minced garlic

2 tablespoons minced fresh basil or 2 teaspoons dried basil

1 tablespoon minced fresh thyme or 1 teaspoon dried thyme

2 large bay leaves

1 teaspoon coarse salt

1 teaspoon freshly milled black pepper

5 tablespoons minced Italian flat-leaf parsley

Put leek, carrots, and celery in a heavy 6-quart saucepan. Add 1 cup of vegetable broth and bring to a boil over medium-high heat. Cook, stirring frequently, until no liquid is left in bottom of pan, about 7 minutes. Add remaining broth, water, brown rice, lentils, tomatoes, garlic, basil, thyme, and bay leaves. Bring to a boil over medium heat. Turn heat to low and simmer, partially covered, stirring occasionally, until lentils and rice are tender, about 55 to 60 minutes. Remove from heat, discard bay leaves, and season with salt and pepper. (Soup can be made up to 3 hours before serving. It will thicken as it stands. If desired, thin it with an additional 1 cup vegetable broth or water before reheating over low heat.) Stir in minced parsley just before serving. Ladle into individual bowls and serve.

Per Serving:	Cal. 261	Carb. 49 gm	Chol. 0 mg
	Fat 1 gm	Prot. 16 gm	Sod. 225 mg

Vegetable Soup with Tubettini

[Minestra di Verdura con Tubettini]

❖

MAKES 7 CUPS, SERVES 4

If tubettini is unavailable, you may substitute ditalini, orzo, or any small pasta for this most nourishing soup.

⅓ cup minced onion
1 tablespoon minced garlic
¼ cup diced peeled carrots
¼ cup chopped celery, strings removed before chopping
5 cups Vegetable Broth, preferably homemade (page 4), or low-sodium canned
3 medium well-ripened plum tomatoes (about 6 ounces), blanched and peeled (see page 126 for technique), cut into ¼-inch dice, with juice included

¼ pound green beans, trimmed and sliced diagonally into 1-inch lengths
¼ cup tubettini (tiny tubular pasta)
3 cups well-packed spinach leaves, thoroughly washed and coarsely chopped
½ teaspoon coarse salt
½ teaspoon freshly milled black pepper
4 teaspoons freshly grated imported Parmesan cheese

Put onion, garlic, carrots, and celery in a heavy 5-quart saucepan. Add 1 cup vegetable broth and bring to a boil over medium-high heat. Cook, stirring frequently, until no liquid is left in bottom of pan, about 7 minutes. Stir in tomatoes and remaining broth. Bring to a boil over medium-high heat. Turn heat to low and simmer, covered, for 20 minutes. Stir in green beans and tubettini. Cook, covered, until pasta is barely al dente, about 7 minutes. Add spinach and continue cooking for an additional 5 minutes. Remove from heat and season with salt and pepper. Ladle into individual bowls, sprinkle each with 1 teaspoon Parmesan cheese and serve.

Per Serving: Cal. 111　Carb. 22 gm　Chol. 1 mg
　　　　　　　Fat 1 gm　Prot. 6 gm　Sod. 288 mg

Zucchini-Rice Soup

[Zuppa di Zucchini e Riso]

MAKES 6 CUPS, SERVES 4

A tasty year-round soup that can be made in less than an hour with the aid of a food processor.

1　tablespoon olive oil
⅓　cup chopped celery, strings removed before chopping
⅓　cup chopped onion
4½　cups Vegetable Broth, preferably homemade (page 4), or low-sodium canned
¼　cup arborio or long-grain rice, picked over to remove any dark grains
2　medium zucchini (about 1 pound), well scrubbed, trimmed, and cut into

strips 1 inch long by ¼ inch wide
2　teaspoons minced fresh thyme or ½ teaspoon dried thyme
½　teaspoon coarse salt
½　teaspoon freshly milled black pepper
4　teaspoons minced Italian flat-leaf parsley, for garnish

In a heavy 5-quart pot, heat olive oil over low heat. Add celery and onion and cook, stirring frequently, until soft, about 5 minutes. If vegetables start to stick, loosen with 2 tablespoons broth. Add broth and bring to a boil over medium heat. As soon as liquid reaches a boil, turn heat to low and stir in rice. Cook, covered, until the rice is barely tender, about 12 to 15 minutes. Stir in zucchini and thyme; cook until zucchini are tender, about 3 minutes. Season with salt and pepper and remove from heat. Ladle into individual bowls, garnish each with 1 teaspoon minced parsley, and serve.

Per Serving: Cal. 127   Carb. 21 gm   Chol. 0 mg
               Fat 4 gm   Prot. 3 gm   Sod. 215 mg

White Bean and Vegetable Soup

[Minestra di Fagioli e Verdura]

MAKES 15 CUPS, SERVES 10

This soup is very substantial, richly satisfying, and an ideal one-dish meal. Like most vegetable soups, this is best made at least 4 hours before serving so that all the flavors have a chance to meld. This soup also freezes very well; it can be put in containers and frozen for up to 3 months. If you wish, each portion may be sprinkled with 1 teaspoon freshly grated Parmesan cheese before serving.

½ pound dried white kidney or Great Northern beans, picked over to remove any foreign matter, rinsed, and drained

2 tablespoons olive oil

1 medium leek (about 5 ounces), root and top trimmed, split in half lengthwise, thoroughly washed, and thinly sliced to make 1½ cups

1 cup diced peeled carrots

½ cup thinly sliced celery, strings removed before slicing

1 can (28 ounces) Italian plum tomatoes, coarsely chopped, juice included (can be chopped in food processor)

1 tablespoon minced garlic

2 tablespoons minced fresh basil or 2 teaspoons dried basil

4 cups shredded savoy cabbage, quartered and cored before shredding

8 cups water

½ pound green beans, trimmed and sliced diagonally into 1-inch lengths

2 medium all-purpose potatoes (8 ounces), peeled and cut into ¾-inch dice

2 medium zucchini (8 ounces), scrubbed, trimmed, and cut into ½-inch dice

½ teaspoon coarse salt

1 teaspoon freshly milled black pepper

1. Place beans in a large bowl, cover with 3 cups cold water, and soak overnight. (Alternatively, you can combine beans and hot tap water in a 5-quart pot and bring to a boil over medium high heat. Boil, uncovered, for 3 minutes. Remove from heat; cover, and let stand for 1 hour.)

2. Drain beans and place in a 5-quart pot. Add 6 cups cold water, cover pot, and bring to a boil over medium heat. Reduce heat to low and cook until beans are tender, about 50 to 60 minutes. Remove from heat and let the beans stand, uncovered.

3. In a heavy 8-quart pot, heat olive oil over low heat. Add leek, carrots, and celery; cook, stirring frequently, just until vegetables are soft, about 5 minutes. If vegetables start to stick to bottom of pan, stir in 2 tablespoons of the juice from tomatoes to loosen. Add

garlic and cook for 1 more minute. Stir in tomatoes and basil; cook, stirring frequently, for 15 minutes. Add cabbage and cook, stirring frequently, until limp, about 5 minutes. Add 8 cups water and bring to a boil over medium heat. As soon as the mixture reaches a boil, cover pot, turn heat to low, and simmer, stirring frequently, for 45 minutes. Stir in green beans and potatoes; cook, covered, for an additional 15 minutes.

4. Drain the white kidney or Great Northern beans in a strainer set over a bowl; reserve cooking liquid. Place half of the beans in food processor with 1 cup reserved cooking liquid and process until puréed, about 30 seconds. Stir the purée and the remaining beans into the soup. Stir in the zucchini, turn heat to low, and simmer, uncovered, for an additional 10 minutes. Season with salt and pepper; remove from heat. (Soup can be made up to 4 hours before serving. It will thicken as it stands. If you like, thin soup with an additional ½ to 1 cup reserved cooking liquid before reheating over low heat.) Ladle into individual bowls and serve.

Per Serving: Cal. 159   Carb. 27 gm   Chol. 0 mg
              Fat 3 gm   Prot. 8 gm   Sod. 227 mg

Pasta

Introduction

Isn't it amazing how the pasta aisles in the supermarkets have expanded over the past decade? This proves that the American's love affair with pasta continues to grow. I can remember that back in the sixties I could only get a variety of different-shaped imported pastas in an Italian specialty store. Fifteen years ago, American pastas were mushy and starchy. As the passion for pasta began to explode in this country, the leading manufacturers decided it was time to compete with the Italians. Today, there are over 150 different shapes of pasta manufactured in the United States. They are made the same as the Italian imported pastas, of 100 percent pure semolina flour and water. I find them as good as the imported brands, and some are even better. When purchasing, make sure that the labels on the boxes read, "Made from pure durum wheat" or "100 percent pure semolina."

On a recent trip to the supermarket, I stopped counting after fifty-six different pasta shapes. There were many small varieties labeled acini di pepe, anellini, ditalini, orzo, pastina, and tubettini. This multitude of mini-shapes—peppercorns, rings, thimbles, rice or melon seeds, stars, and tubes—are used for soups or as a side dish. Then I started counting the long varieties, including capellini, vermicelli, linguine, spaghettini, spaghetti, bucatini, perciatelli, curly and flat lasagne. Many of these varieties have numbers to differentiate from very fine to not so fine, narrow to wide, and thin to thick. The truly imaginative shapes are the shells, bows, tubes, twists, and curls with melodious names like conchiglie, farfalle, penne rigati, rigatoni, ziti, fusilli, rotelle, and ricciolini. We could eat this versatile, economical food, rich in carbohydrates and a good source of protein, every day for five months without repeating a shape. The different shapes give different taste or "mouth feel" to a dish. A good general rule of thumb is that thinner pastas, such as capellini, linguine, spaghettini, and vermicelli are perfect vehicles for the Tomato-Basil Sauce (page 24) or the light, creamy, and thin vegetable sauces. Spaghettini or vermicelli is also excellent for making frittatas. This very thin pasta bonds better with vegetables in the skillet than the broader or thicker shapes. The thicker cuts such as conchiglie, farfalle, fusilli, penne, rotelle, or ziti are paired with the assertive bean or vegetable sauces, especially when the vegetables are cut to match the size of the pasta.

Perfectly cooked pasta should be tender but still firm to the bite (al dente). Taste the pasta often during cooking for doneness. The only time you should rinse pasta is if you are making lasagne, which must be quickly precooked, rinsed to stop the cooking, and drained well before layering. Once all other types of pastas are cooked, drain thoroughly, transfer to a warm bowl or back into the pot in which the pasta was cooked, and toss immediately with the amount of sauce specified in each recipe.

Couscous is just beginning to gain popularity in this country. I was first introduced to these coarsely ground pellets of durum wheat (semolina) by my Sicilian mother-in-law. She always purchased couscous loose in Middle Eastern stores. It was cooked in the authentic time-consuming way, by steaming the pellets, and took at least two hours to prepare. It was always served as a main course for lunch or at dinner as an accompaniment to many of her favorite fish dishes. For today's life-style, I have chosen to use the quick-cooking variety, which is ready in a matter of minutes. This type of couscous is imported from the Middle East, France, and Italy and is available in supermarkets, gourmet shops, and Italian specialty stores.

The next time you're looking for a different grain to serve, consider couscous. And when pasta is being planned, try a new shape with a different sauce. The following recipes are simple to prepare. Many can be cooked while the water is coming to a boil, so that dinner can be on the table in less than an hour. Try one of the following recipes when you want to put something nutritious and memorable on your table.

Tomato-Basil Sauce

[Salsa di Pomodoro]

3 CUPS

This basic tomato sauce is incorporated into several recipes in this book, so you may want to double the recipe and freeze half. This sauce can be kept frozen up to 2 months. If doubling the recipe, increase cooking time to 45 minutes.

1½ tablespoons olive oil
⅓ cup minced red onion
⅓ cup finely minced peeled carrot
2 teaspoons minced garlic
1 can (28 ounces) Italian plum tomatoes with tomato purée, finely chopped, purée included (can be chopped in food processor)

¼ teaspoon freshly grated nutmeg
½ teaspoon coarse salt
½ teaspoon freshly milled black pepper
½ teaspoon sugar
2 tablespoons minced fresh basil or 2 teaspoons dried basil

In a 12-inch nonstick skillet, heat olive oil over low heat. Add onion and carrot; cook, stirring constantly, until soft but not brown, about 4 minutes. Add garlic and continue to cook for an additional minute. Stir in tomatoes, nutmeg, salt, pepper, sugar, and basil. Turn heat to high and bring to a boil. Reduce heat to medium and cook, stirring frequently, until slightly thickened, about 20 minutes. Remove from heat, cover pan, and let sauce rest for at least 1 hour before using.

Per ½ cup: Cal. 76   Carb. 10 gm   Chol. 0 mg
            Fat 3 gm   Prot. 2 gm   Sod. 335 mg

Capellini with Tomato-Basil Sauce

[Capellini con Salsa di Pomodoro]

SERVES 6

This flavorful sauce is equally delectable with other types of thin pasta, such as spaghettini, vermicelli, and angel hair.

Tomato-Basil Sauce (page 24)
3 tablespoons minced Italian flat-leaf parsley
1 pound capellini
2 teaspoons coarse salt
¼ cup grated imported pecorino romano cheese, for serving

1. Prepare sauce 2 hours before cooking pasta. Reheat sauce over low heat while cooking pasta. Stir parsley into sauce just before tossing with pasta.
2. Cook pasta in 6 quarts boiling water with 2 teaspoons coarse salt until al dente. Drain pasta in colander, transfer to bowl, and toss with ¾ of the sauce. Spoon remaining sauce on top; serve with pecorino romano cheese.

Per Serving: Cal. 364   Carb. 67 gm   Chol. 2 mg
              Fat 5 gm   Prot. 12 gm   Sod. 629 mg

Conchiglie with Peas and Red Kidney Beans

[Conchiglie con Piselle e Fagioli]

❖

SERVES 6

This is one pasta dish to make when you are pressed for time and want dinner served in less than 30 minutes. Allowing this dish to rest before serving enhances the flavor by letting the pasta absorb most of the broth. If you wish, you may sprinkle a little grated pecorino romano cheese over each serving.

1 tablespoon olive oil	(page 4), or low-sodium
½ cup minced red onion	canned
2 teaspoons minced garlic	1 can (16 ounces) dark red
1 package (9 ounces) tiny	kidney beans, rinsed and
frozen peas, defrosted and	well drained
well drained	2½ teaspoons coarse salt
1 tablespoon minced fresh	½ teaspoon freshly milled
sage or 1 teaspoon	black pepper
crumbled dried sage	1 pound conchiglie (medium
½ teaspoon crushed fennel seed	size shells)
1 cup Vegetable Broth,	¼ cup minced Italian flat-leaf
preferably homemade	parsley

1. In a heavy 3-quart saucepan, heat olive oil over low heat. Add onion and cook, stirring frequently, until slightly softened, about 2 minutes. Add garlic and continue cooking, stirring frequently until slightly softened, about 1 minute. Stir in peas, sage, fennel seed, and broth. Cook, covered, until peas are barely tender, about 2 minutes. Stir in kidney beans, ½ teaspoon of the salt, and pepper. Cook, covered, for an additional 5 minutes.

2. Cook pasta in 6 quarts of boiling water with remaining 2 teaspoons coarse salt until al dente. Drain pasta in colander and return to pot in which it was boiled. Stir in pea mixture, cover pot, and let rest for 5 minutes before serving. Stir in parsley; ladle into bowls and serve.

Per Serving: Cal. 396   Carb. 73 gm   Chol. 0 mg
               Fat 4 gm   Prot. 16 gm   Sod. 284 mg

Couscous with Peas and Mint

[Cùscusu con Piselle e Menta]

SERVES 6

This light grain is simple to prepare and as versatile as pasta. Serve with Veggie Burgers with Tomato-Thyme Sauce (page 95) and Broccoli Salad with Lemon-Honey Dressing (page 140).

1 tablespoon olive oil	1½ cups quick-cooking couscous
½ cup thinly sliced scallions	½ teaspoon coarse salt
3 cups Vegetable Broth, preferably homemade (page 4), or low-sodium canned	½ teaspoon freshly milled white pepper
1 package (10 ounces) tiny frozen peas, defrosted and well drained	3 tablespoons minced fresh mint or 1½ teaspoons dried mint

In a heavy 3½-quart saucepan, heat olive oil over medium heat. Add scallions and cook, stirring frequently, until barely tender, about 1 minute. Add vegetable broth, cover pan, turn heat to high, and bring to a boil. Stir in peas and cook until barely tender, about 1 minute. Slowly pour in couscous and cook, stirring vigorously with wooden spoon, until almost all of the broth is absorbed, about 30 seconds. Season with salt and pepper; remove from heat. Cover pan and let stand for 8 to 10 minutes. Fluff couscous with two forks, stir in mint, transfer to bowl, and serve.

Per Serving: Cal. 241   Carb. 45 gm   Chol. 0 mg
              Fat 3 gm   Prot. 9 gm   Sod. 200 mg

Farfalle with Broccoli di Rape

[Farfalle con Broccoletti di Rape]

SERVES 6

This is one of my favorite pasta dishes to make whenever I can find bunches of broccoli di rape with firm small stems and bright green buds.

2 large bunches broccoli di rape (about 2 pounds)	2½ teaspoons coarse salt
1 tablespoon extra virgin olive oil	½ teaspoon crushed red pepper flakes
3 large cloves garlic, peeled and sliced paper-thin	1 pound farfalle (bow ties)
	¼ cup grated imported pecorino romano cheese

1. Remove any discolored leaves from broccoli di rape. Cut off about ½ inch of tough bottom stems and discard. Wash several times in tepid water to remove sand and drain in colander. Cut off stems of broccoli di rape up to within about 1 inch of leaves. With a sharp knife, peel away the outer layer of stem pieces. (Once peeled and

cooked, the stems are just as tender as the florets.) Cut stems and tops of broccoli di rape into 2-inch lengths.

2. In a heavy 5-quart saucepan, heat olive oil over low heat. Add garlic and sauté until very lightly golden. Remove pan from heat. With a slotted spoon, remove garlic and transfer to small plate.

3. Place broccoli di rape in pan and scatter garlic over leaves. Cover pan and cook over medium heat, stirring once or twice, until stems are extremely tender, about 5 minutes. Season with ½ teaspoon of the salt, and crushed red pepper flakes.

4. Meanwhile, cook pasta in 6 quarts of boiling water with remaining 2 teaspoons coarse salt until al dente. Before draining pasta, remove about ½ cup of the pasta water and set aside. Drain pasta in colander, transfer to bowl, and toss with ¾ of the broccoli di rape mixture and about 6 tablespoons of the pasta water to loosen. Spoon remaining broccoli di rape mixture over top. Serve with pecorino romano cheese.

Per Serving: Cal. 360   Carb. 64 gm   Chol. 5 mg
               Fat 5 gm   Prot. 15 gm   Sod. 526 mg

Fusilli with Cauliflower and Tomato

[Fusilli con Cavolfiore e Pomodoro]

SERVES 6

Fusilli comes in two shapes—quite different but given the same name. One is a long twisted shape that looks like a corkscrew, and the other a short spiral. The one you want for this Sicilian classic is the short spiral type. This sauce is also excellent spooned over bowls of hot polenta.

1	large head cauliflower (about 2 pounds)		cut into ½-inch dice with juice included
2½	teaspoons coarse salt	2	tablespoons minced fresh
1	tablespoon olive oil		basil or 2 teaspoons dried
1	medium leek (5 ounces), root and top trimmed, split in half lengthwise, thoroughly washed, and thinly sliced to make 1 cup		basil
		½	teaspoon freshly milled black pepper
		3	tablespoons minced Italian flat-leaf parsley
12	large well-ripened plum tomatoes (2 pounds), blanched, peeled (see page 126 for technique),	1	pound short fusilli spirals
		¼	cup freshly grated imported Parmesan cheese

1. Remove florets from cauliflower, leaving ½ inch of stems. Cut or break into 1-inch pieces. Wash in cold water and drain.
2. Bring 6 quarts of water to a boil. Add 2 teaspoons of the coarse salt and the cauliflower florets. Boil until barely tender, about 5 minutes. Using a slotted spoon, transfer florets to a colander. Reserve liquid for cooking pasta.
3. In a 12-inch nonstick skillet, heat olive oil over medium heat. Add leek and sauté, stirring once or twice, until slightly softened, about 4 minutes. Add tomatoes, basil, remaining ½ teaspoon salt, and pepper. Cook sauce, partially covered, stirring frequently for 10 minutes. Add cauliflower and cook uncovered, stirring frequently until cauliflower is extremely tender, about 5 minutes. Remove from heat and stir in parsley.
4. Meanwhile, return water to a boil. Add pasta and cook until al dente. Drain pasta in a colander, transfer to a bowl and toss with ¾ of the sauce. Spoon remaining sauce on top. Serve with freshly grated Parmesan cheese.

Per Serving:	Cal. 362	Carb. 68 gm	Chol. 2 mg
	Fat 5 gm	Prot. 13 gm	Sod. 425 mg

Lemon Couscous Salad with Spinach

[Insalata di Cùscusu]

SERVES 6

This flavorful salad is quick to prepare on those hot summer days when you don't want to spend hours in the kitchen. Serve with Roasted Beet Salad (page 139) and Grilled White Eggplant (page 128) to complete the meal.

3	cups water	1½	tablespoons extra virgin olive oil
1½	cups quick-cooking couscous	1	tablespoon minced fresh thyme or 1 teaspoon dried thyme
3	tablespoons strained fresh lemon juice		
⅓	cup Vegetable Broth, preferably homemade (page 4), or low-sodium canned	2	cups well-packed spinach leaves, thoroughly washed, spun dry, and coarsely chopped
½	teaspoon coarse salt		
½	teaspoon freshly milled white pepper	½	cup thinly sliced scallions

1. In a heavy 3½-quart saucepan, bring water to a boil over high heat. Slowly pour in couscous and cook, stirring vigorously with wooden spoon, until almost all of the water is absorbed, about 30 seconds. Remove pan from heat and let couscous stand, covered, for 15 minutes. Fluff couscous with two forks and transfer to deep bowl.
2. In a small bowl, combine lemon juice, broth, salt, and pepper. Stir with fork or small whisk to combine. Add extra virgin olive oil and thyme; whisk until dressing is well blended. Drizzle dressing over couscous and toss until well combined. Cover with plastic wrap and let cool to room temperature. Fluff with two forks once again and

stir in spinach and scallions. (Salad may be prepared up to 2 hours before serving. Cover with plastic wrap and refrigerate until needed. Fluff with two forks just before serving.)

Per Serving: Cal. 271   Carb. 39 gm   Chol. 0 mg
              Fat 4 gm   Prot. 7 gm   Sod. 155 mg

Linguine with Sweet Onions and Lemon

[Linguine con Cipolle e Limone]

SERVES 6

An excellent sauce to make in spring when Vidalia onions are abundant at the market. If Vidalia onions are unavailable, Walla Wallas or Texas Whites may be substituted.

1 large lemon (4 ounces)	2½ teaspoons coarse salt
1 tablespoon olive oil	1 teaspoon freshly milled black pepper
2 large Vidalia onions (1¼ pounds), peeled, halved, cored, and sliced lengthwise (2½ cups)	1 pound linguine
	¼ cup finely snipped fresh chives or top tender green part of scallions, for garnish
1¼ cups Vegetable Broth, preferably homemade (page 4), or low-sodium canned	¼ cup freshly grated imported Parmesan cheese

1. Using a vegetable peeler, remove zest (thin outer peel with no white pith) from lemon and cut into ⅛-inch julienne strips to make ¼ cup loosely packed. Place zest in a small saucepan and cover with 1 inch of water. Bring to a boil; drain. Repeat twice. Thoroughly blot zest dry with paper towels after third blanching and reserve for garnish. Squeeze juice from lemon and measure out ¼ cup for sauce.
2. In a 12-inch nonstick skillet, heat olive oil over medium-low heat. Add onions and sauté until tender-crisp, about 5 minutes. If onions start to stick to bottom of pan, stir in 2 tablespoons vegetable broth to loosen. Add vegetable broth and cook over low heat, stirring frequently, until onions are extremely soft and translucent, about 8 minutes. Remove from heat, stir in lemon juice, and season with ½ teaspoon of the salt, and pepper.
3. Cook pasta in 6 quarts boiling water with remaining 2 teaspoons coarse salt until al dente. Drain pasta in colander, transfer to bowl, and toss with onion mixture. Garnish with snipped chives and lemon zest. Serve with freshly grated Parmesan cheese.

Per Serving: Cal. 357 Carb. 68 gm Chol. 2 gm
              Fat 4 gm Prot. 12 gm Sod. 415 mg

Orzo Pilaf with Red Pepper

[Orzo alla Palmina]

SERVES 4

Orzo, a rice-shaped pasta, is sold in most supermarkets or Italian specialty stores. Good accompaniments to this side dish would be Yellow Wax Beans with Olives and Sage (page 130) and Broccoli Salad with Lemon-Honey Dressing (page 140).

2 teaspoons olive oil	(page 4), or low-sodium
⅓ cup chopped onion	canned
1 large red bell pepper, halved, cored, seeded, deribbed, and cut into ¼-inch dice	1¼ cups orzo
	½ teaspoon coarse salt
	½ teaspoon freshly milled white pepper
3 cups Vegetable Broth, preferably homemade	3 tablespoons minced Italian flat-leaf parsley

Heat olive oil in a heavy 3½-quart saucepan over medium heat. Add onion and red pepper and sauté, stirring frequently, until tender-crisp, about 2 minutes. Add broth and bring to a boil over high heat. Stir in orzo and reduce heat to low. Cover and simmer, stirring frequently, until orzo is tender and has absorbed all the broth, about 15 to 20 minutes. Remove from heat, season with salt and pepper, and stir in parsley. Transfer to a bowl and serve.

Per Serving:	Cal. 286	Carb. 54 gm	Chol. 0 mg
	Fat 3 gm	Prot. 9 gm	Sod. 202 mg

Penne with Tomato and Pole Beans

[Penne con Pomodoro e Fagiolini Verdi]

SERVES 6

Pole beans are sometimes labeled Italian broad beans. If pole beans are unavailable, substitute green beans for this simple yet satisfying pasta entrée.

1½ pounds pole beans, washed and trimmed
1 tablespoon olive oil
¾ cup thinly sliced scallions
5 medium well-ripened round tomatoes (about ¼ pound), blanched, peeled (see page 126 for technique), and coarsely chopped with juice included

1½ tablespoons minced fresh sage or 1½ teaspoons crumbled dried sage
3 large bay leaves
2½ teaspoons coarse salt
1 teaspoon freshly milled black pepper
1 pound penne rigati (or any medium-size tubular pasta)
¼ cup grated imported pecorino romano cheese

1. Bring 6 quarts of water to a boil. Add beans and cook until barely tender, about 3 minutes. Using a slotted spoon, transfer beans to colander and drain thoroughly. When cool enough to handle, slice beans diagonally into 1-inch lengths. Reserve water for cooking pasta.
2. Heat olive oil in a 12-inch nonstick skillet over medium heat. Add scallions and sauté, stirring constantly, until barely tender, about 1 minute. Add tomatoes, sage, bay leaves, ½ teaspoon of the salt, and pepper. Bring sauce to a boil over high heat. As soon as it reaches a boil, reduce heat to low and cook, stirring frequently with wooden spoon, for 10 minutes. Add beans and mix well with spoon. Cook, partially covered, stirring frequently, until beans are tender, about 10 minutes. Remove bay leaves from sauce just before tossing with pasta.
3. Bring water in which beans were cooked back to a boil. Add remaining 2 teaspoons coarse salt and cook pasta until al dente. Drain pasta in colander and transfer to a bowl. Toss pasta with ¾ of the sauce; spoon remaining sauce on top. Serve with pecorino romano cheese.

Per Serving: Cal. 373   Carb. 69 gm   Chol. 3 mg
              Fat 5 gm   Prot. 13 gm   Sod. 461 mg

Ricotta Gnocchi with Tomato-Basil Sauce

[Gnocchi con Salsa di Pomodoro]

❖

SERVES 6

This recipe was created by my dear friend and colleague, Arlene Coria Ward. Shaping gnocchi is a fun hands-on project to share with family and friends, especially if you are making more than one batch of dough. My grandsons, John Paul and Colin, love helping to roll the dough off a fork to form these crescent-shaped dumplings.

Tomato-Basil Sauce (page 24)	2½ teaspoons coarse salt
2 tablespoons minced Italian flat-leaf parsley	1¾ to 2 cups all-purpose unbleached flour
1 cup part-skim ricotta cheese	¼ cup freshly grated imported Parmesan cheese

1. Prepare sauce 2 hours before cooking gnocchi, and reheat it over low heat while cooking gnocchi. Stir parsley into sauce just before tossing with gnocchi.

2. Place ricotta, ½ teaspoon salt, and 1¾ cups flour in food processor fitted with metal blade. Process by pulsing with quick on/off action until mixture resembles little beads of cheese, about 30 seconds. Stop machine and remove about 1 tablespoon of dough. With the palms of your hands, roll into a ball. At this point dough should hold together. If dough is too wet and doesn't form a ball, add additional flour, 1 tablespoon at a time, and continue pulsing with quick on/off action for 20 seconds after each addition. Once dough begins to hold together, process just until it starts to mass together into a ball, about 30 seconds. Transfer dough to a lightly floured sur-

face and knead until slightly sticky to the touch. Shape into a cylinder about 8 inches long and 3 inches thick. Lightly dust with flour, place in a deep bowl, and cover with plastic wrap. Let dough rest for at least 40 minutes before shaping.

3. Slice cylinder into 7 even slices. Remove 1 slice of dough and place on a lightly floured surface. Cover remaining slices with a towel to prevent them from drying. With the palms of your hands, roll dough into a rope about ½-inch thick. Cut rope into ¾-inch lengths. Place each piece of dough on the inside (curved side) of a 4-pronged fork. With your index and middle finger lightly press and roll dough along the inside curve of fork. As you press and roll, let the gnocchi drop onto a lightly floured dish towel, about ½ inch apart, to prevent them from sticking together. Each gnocchi should be somewhat of a crescent shape, with the ridge on the outside and a slight impression on the inside formed by your fingertips. Repeat rolling and cutting with remaining slices of dough.

4. Bring 6 quarts of water to a boil and add remaining 2 teaspoons coarse salt. Drop gnocchi, a few at a time, into boiling water, and cook until they all rise to the surface. Continue cooking until tender, about 3 to 5 minutes. Drain in colander, transfer to bowl, and toss gently with ¾ of the sauce. Spoon remaining sauce on top and serve with Parmesan cheese.

Per Serving: Cal. 260   Carb. 39 gm   Chol. 15 mg.
                 Fat 6 gm   Prot. 11 gm   Sod. 414 mg

Rotelle with Tomato, Zucchini, Olives, and Goat Cheese

[Pasta alla Emilia]

❖

SERVES 6

This is a lightened version of a recipe I received from my friend Emi Havas. The goat cheese adds a creamy texture to the pasta, while the chewy bits of olives add intensified flavor.

Tomato-Basil Sauce
(page 24)
3 medium zucchini (about
1½ pounds), well scrubbed,
trimmed, cut lengthwise,
and sliced crosswise into
½-inch pieces
¼ cup oil-cured olives, pitted
and coarsely chopped

1 pound rotelle or fusilli
pasta
2 teaspoons coarse salt
2 ounces mild goat cheese,
crumbled
½ cup minced Italian flat-leaf
parsley

1. Prepare sauce. As soon as sauce has finished cooking, stir in zucchini. Cook, partially covered, stirring once or twice, until tender, about 5 minutes. Stir in olives and remove from heat. (Sauce can be prepared up to 3 hours ahead. Reheat, covered, over low heat while cooking pasta.)

2. Cook pasta in 6 quarts of boiling water with 2 teaspoons coarse salt until al dente. Drain pasta in colander and return to pot in which it was boiled. Add sauce and stir to combine. Stir in goat cheese and parsley. Cover and let stand for 5 minutes before serving. Transfer to pasta bowls and serve.

Per Serving: Cal. 410 Carb. 72 gm Chol. 8 mg
              Fat 8 gm Prot. 14 gm Sod. 600 mg

Spaghettini with Creamy Spinach Pesto

[Spaghettini con Pesto Toscano]

SERVES 6

With the aid of a food processor, this Tuscan-style pasta dish is ready to serve in less than 30 minutes. If you like, you can make a creamy basil pesto sauce by replacing the 4 cups of spinach with 2 cups well-packed fresh basil leaves.

4   cups well-packed spinach leaves, thoroughly washed and spun dry
½   cups scallions, white part and 3 inches of green, cut into ½-inch lengths
¼   cup Italian flat-leaf parsley
¾   cup Vegetable Broth, preferably homemade (page 4), or low-sodium canned

1   cup part-skim ricotta cheese
3   tablespoons freshly grated imported Parmesan cheese
1   tablespoon grated lemon zest
2½ teaspoons coarse salt
½   teaspoon freshly milled black pepper
1   pound spaghettini

1. Put spinach leaves, scallions, parsley, and vegetable broth in food processor. Process until coarsely chopped, about 30 seconds, stopping machine once to scrape down inside work bowl with plastic spatula. Add ricotta, Parmesan cheese, lemon zest, ½ teaspoon of the salt, and pepper. Process until pesto is smooth and creamy, about 20 seconds.
2. Cook pasta in 6 quarts boiling water with remaining 2 teaspoons

coarse salt until al dente. Drain pasta in colander and return to pot in which it was boiled. Add pesto and toss to combine. Heat over low heat, stirring constantly, until warmed through. Transfer to pasta bowls and serve.

Per Serving: Cal. 355   Carb. 63 gm   Chol. 14 mg.
              Fat 5 gm   Prot. 17 gm   Sod. 500 mg

$\mathcal{T}$ricolor $\mathcal{P}$asta $\mathcal{S}$alad

[Insalata alla Louisa]

SERVES 8

This colorful combination is best served at room temperature no longer than 2 hours after it is made, so that the pasta remains moist. This recipe is an adaptation of one I received from my twin sister, Louisa.

½ cup sun-dried tomatoes, not packed in oil

4 cups bite-size broccoli florets, with ½ inch of stems included, washed and drained

3 small yellow squash (about 12 ounces), scrubbed, trimmed, quartered lengthwise, and sliced crosswise into ½-inch lengths

1 pound tricolor rotelle or fusilli

½ cup sliced scallions (white part and 2 inches of green), sliced into ½-inch lengths

¼ cup well-packed fresh basil leaves or 2 teaspoons dried basil

⅓ cup well-packed Italian flat-leaf parsley

2 tablespoons imported white wine vinegar

1 tablespoon extra virgin olive oil

2½ teaspoons coarse salt

½ teaspoon freshly milled black pepper

¼ cup snipped green tops of scallions, for garnish

1. Place sun-dried tomatoes in a bowl and pour on boiling water to cover. Let stand 2 minutes to soften; drain thoroughly. When cool enough to handle, slice diagonally into ½-inch strips; set aside.
2. Put broccoli florets in a steamer with 1 inch of water in bottom of 5-quart saucepan. Place sliced yellow squash in between florets. Cook, covered, over medium-high heat until vegetables are tender, about 5 minutes. Remove steamer and let vegetables cool to room temperature. Transfer to bowl, combine with sun-dried tomatoes, and cover with plastic wrap. Measure out 1 cup of liquid from bottom of saucepan and reserve for dressing.
3. Cook pasta in 6 quarts boiling water with 2 teaspoons of the coarse salt until al dente. Drain in colander and transfer to bowl.
4. While pasta is cooking, place scallions, basil, and parsley in food processor; process until coarsely chopped, about 30 seconds. Add reserved cooking liquid, vinegar, extra virgin olive oil, remaining ½ teaspoon coarse salt, and pepper; process until dressing is well blended, about 30 seconds. Toss dressing with hot pasta, cover with plastic wrap, and let cool to room temperature. Add vegetables and toss to combine. (Pasta salad can be made up to 2 hours before serving. Cover with plastic wrap and leave at room temperature.) When ready to serve, toss again and garnish with snipped scallions.

Per Serving: Cal. 270   Carb. 52 gm   Chol. 0 mg
              Fat 3 gm   Prot. 11 gm   Sod. 334 mg

Vermicelli Frittata with Zucchini and Mushrooms

[Frittata alla Nonna]

✦

8 SLICES

My grandmother, Nonna Louisa, always made frittatas with pasta that had already been mixed with sauce or vegetables and left over from the previous day. For each cup of mixed pasta, blend in either ¼ cup egg substitute or 1 large egg, well beaten, and follow the procedure given below for cooking frittata. If Asiago cheese in unavailable, substitute imported Parmesan cheese.

4 small zucchini (1 pound), well scrubbed

4 teaspoons olive oil

½ cup thinly sliced shallots

6 ounces crimini or white mushrooms, stemmed, wiped, and thinly sliced

8 ounces vermicelli

2½ teaspoons coarse salt

12 ounces fat-free egg substitute, at room temperature

3 tablespoons freshly grated mellow Asiago cheese

1 tablespoon minced fresh thyme or 1 teaspoon dried thyme

¼ cup minced Italian flat-leaf parsley

½ teaspoon freshly milled black pepper

1. Cook zucchini in 4 quarts boiling water until barely tender, about 3 minutes. With a slotted spoon, remove zucchini and drain in colander. When cool enough to handle, trim ends of zucchini and discard. Halve zucchini lengthwise and slice into ½-inch pieces; set aside. Reserve water for cooking pasta.
2. In a 12-inch nonstick skillet, heat 2 teaspoons olive oil over medium heat. Add shallots and cook, stirring frequently, until

lightly golden, about 5 minutes. Add mushrooms and cook, stirring frequently, until tender, about 2 minutes. Stir in zucchini and cook until incorporated into shallots and mushrooms, about 1 minute. Transfer vegetable mixture to a deep bowl and allow to cool to room temperature.

3. Return cooking water to a boil. Break vermicelli in half and cook with 2 teaspoons of the coarse salt until very firm to the bite. Drain in colander, rinse under cold water, and drain again; toss gently with vegetable mixture.

4. In a medium bowl, beat egg substitute, cheese, thyme, parsley, remaining ½ teaspoon coarse salt, and pepper. Pour over pasta mixture and combine well with two forks.

5. Adjust oven rack to upper third of oven and preheat to broil setting.

6. In same skillet, heat remaining 2 teaspoons of olive oil over medium heat. Add entire mixture and spread evenly with two forks. Partially cover pan, turn heat to medium, and cook, without stirring, until frittata is almost cooked through on surface, and bottom of frittata is lightly golden, about 8 minutes. (Check by lifting edge with a narrow metal spatula.)

7. Wrap a double layer of aluminum foil around handle of skillet to prevent it from burning under broiler. Place pan in oven and broil until surface of frittata is golden brown, about 5 to 7 minutes. (Watch carefully so that surface does not burn.) Invert frittata onto large round platter and let cool for at least 8 minutes before slicing into wedges. Frittata can be served warm or at room temperature.

Per Slice: Cal. 176   Carb. 26 gm   Chol. 2 mg
                Fat 3 gm   Prot. 10 gm   Sod. 291 mg

Vegetable Lasagne with Tomato-Basil Sauce

[Lasagne Riccie con Verdure e Salsa di Pomodoro]

SERVES 12

Here is a great do-ahead dish for entertaining. For ease of preparation, the sauce can be made up 2 days ahead and lasagne can be assembled a day in advance and refrigerated. Remove from refrigerator 1 hour before baking.

Tomato-Basil Sauce (page 24)

1 small purple eggplant (about 1¼ pounds) washed, ends trimmed, peeled, and sliced into ¼-inch rounds

1 tablespoon plus 2 teaspoons coarse salt

2 teaspoons olive oil

1 large zucchini (12 ounces), well scrubbed and trimmed

5 medium carrots (10 ounces), trimmed and peeled

1 container (15 ounces) part-skim ricotta cheese

2 ounces part-skim mozzarella cheese, cut into ½-inch cubes (½ cup)

7 tablespoons freshly grated imported Parmesan cheese

¼ cup well-packed Italian flat-leaf parsley

½ teaspoon freshly milled black pepper

2 large egg whites, or ¼ cup fat-free egg substitute

1 pound curly lasagne noodles (18 strips)

1. Prepare sauce 3 hours ahead, or make up to 2 days in advance and refrigerate before assembling lasagne.

2. Sprinkle eggplant slices on both sides with 1 tablespoon of the salt and layer in colander. Set colander over a deep plate. Place an inverted plate on top of slices, weight, and drain for 30 minutes (a 28-ounce can of tomatoes works well for weighting). After draining, thoroughly rinse slices under cold running water. Squeeze,

2 slices at a time, to get rid of excess moisture; thoroughly blot dry with paper towels.

3. Adjust oven rack 4 inches from heat source and preheat to broil setting. Lightly grease surface of broiler rack (set over broiler pan) with vegetable cooking spray.

4. Arrange eggplant in single layer in pan. Brush surface of eggplant with the olive oil. Broil until lightly golden and tender, about 3 minutes on each side; set aside.

5. Cook zucchini and carrots in 2 quarts of boiling water until very tender, about 5 minutes. Rinse under cold water and drain. Slice zucchini and carrots on a diagonal into ¼-inch slices; separate and set aside.

6. Put ricotta, mozzarella, 5 tablespoons of Parmesan cheese, parsley, pepper, and egg whites in food processor. Process until mozzarella is coarsely grated and parsley is finely minced, about 20 seconds; transfer to bowl.

7. Bring 6 quarts of water to a boil and add remaining 2 teaspoons coarse salt. Drop lasagna strips, one at a time, into boiling water. (Dropping one at a time will prevent them from sticking together.) Cook until barely tender, about 4 minutes. Drain in colander, refresh under cold water, and drain again.

8. Cover work surface with a large dish towel. Place lasagna strips on work surface in single layer. Evenly spread ½ cup of sauce in bottom of a 9 X 13 X 2–inch ovenproof baking dish. Overlap 5 strips of pasta over sauce. Spread ⅓ of the cheese mixture over pasta. Arrange carrots atop. Spread ½ cup sauce over carrot layer. Overlap 4 strips of pasta as next layer. Spread with ⅓ of cheese mixture. Arrange zucchini atop. Spread ½ cup sauce over zucchini layer. Overlap another 4 strips of pasta and spread with remaining cheese mixture. Arrange eggplant atop. Spread ½ cup sauce over eggplant layer. Overlap 5 remaining strips of pasta atop. Spread remaining sauce over pasta and sprinkle with remaining 2 tablespoons Parmesan cheese. Place a lightly oiled piece of parchment paper over lasagne and cover top of dish with heavy-duty foil. Set aside until oven is hot.

9. Adjust oven rack to center of oven and preheat to 350°F. Bake lasagne for 1 hour and 20 minutes. Remove from oven and let rest,

covered, for at least 20 minutes before serving. To serve, cut into squares and lift out with metal spatula.

Per Serving: Cal. 278   Carb. 40 gm. Chol. 16 mg.
              Fat 7 gm   Prot. 13 gm   Sod. 436 gm

Whole-Wheat Spaghetti with Mushrooms

[Spaghetti alla Mama]

SERVES 6

This is an adaptation of a dish my mother frequently served during the winter months. Porcini mushrooms accentuate the robust flavor of this hearty pasta dish. Dried porcini mushrooms and whole-wheat pasta are available in many supermarkets and Italian specialty stores.

½ ounce dried porcini mushrooms
1 tablespoon olive oil
½ cup minced red onion
2 teaspoons minced garlic
1 pound white mushrooms, trimmed, wiped, and thinly sliced
1 tablespoon minced fresh thyme or 1 teaspoon dried thyme

2½ teaspoons coarse salt
½ teaspoon freshly milled black pepper
1 pound whole-wheat spaghetti
¼ cup minced Italian flat-leaf parsley, for garnish
¼ cup freshly grated imported Parmesan cheese

1. Soak the dried porcini mushrooms in 1 cup warm water for 30 minutes. Drain mushrooms in strainer set over a bowl. Rinse mush-

rooms in cold water, blot dry, and chop fine; set aside. Pour mushroom liquid through strainer lined with paper towel to remove sand; reserve liquid for sauce.

2. In a 12-inch nonstick skillet, heat olive oil, over medium heat. Add onion and cook until lightly golden, about 6 minutes. Add garlic and cook, stirring frequently, for another minute. Stir in white mushrooms and sauté, stirring frequently, until tender, about 5 minutes. Add the chopped porcini mushrooms, reserved soaking liquid, and thyme; cook for an additional 5 minutes. Season with ½ teaspoon of the salt, and pepper; remove from heat.

3. Cook pasta in 6 quarts boiling water with remaining 2 teaspoons coarse salt until al dente. Drain pasta in colander and transfer to bowl. Toss pasta with ¾ of the sauce. Spoon remaining sauce on top, garnish with parsley, and serve topped with Parmesan cheese.

Per Serving: Cal. 325   Carb. 63 gm   Chol. 2 mg
              Fat 4 gm   Prot. 14 gm   Sod. 469 mg

Ziti with Roasted Yellow Peppers and Sun-Dried Tomatoes

[Ziti alla Costanza]

❖

SERVES 6

I don't know of anyone in my family who loves pasta more than my cousin Connie Benincasa Seaman. This is one of her favorite pasta recipes, which she serves when firm yellow bell peppers are available at the market. Once the peppers are roasted, this pasta dish takes less than 30 minutes to prepare.

1 tablespoon extra virgin olive oil	sliced lengthwise into ½-inch strips
½ cup minced shallots	3 tablespoons minced fresh basil
1 cup Vegetable Broth, preferably homemade (page 4), or low-sodium canned	2½ teaspoons coarse salt
	½ teaspoon freshly milled black pepper
⅓ cup sun-dried tomatoes not packed in oil, coarsely chopped	1 pound ziti
	6 large basil leaves, stacked and sliced into thin strips, for garnish
4 large firm yellow bell peppers (2 pounds), roasted and peeled (see page 125 for technique),	¼ cup freshly grated imported Parmesan cheese

1. In a 12-inch nonstick skillet, heat extra virgin olive oil over low heat. Add shallots and sauté until lightly golden, about 1 minute. Stir in vegetable broth and sun-dried tomatoes. Turn heat up to medium and cook, stirring frequently, until sun-dried tomatoes are

softened, about 2 minutes. Add yellow peppers and continue cooking, stirring once or twice, until heated, about 1 minute. Stir in basil, season with ½ teaspoon of the salt, and pepper, and remove from heat.

2. While vegetable mixture is cooking, cook pasta in 6 quarts boiling water with remaining 2 teaspoons coarse salt until al dente. Drain in colander and transfer to bowl. Toss with ¾ of the vegetable mixture and spoon remaining vegetable mixture on top. Garnish with basil and serve with Parmesan cheese.

Per Serving: Cal. 372   Carb. 71 gm   Chol. 2 mg
                    Fat 4 gm   Prot. 13 gm   Sod. 413 mg

Polenta

Polenta, cooked yellow cornmeal, is served in many parts of Italy as an alternative to pasta. When I was a child growing up during the depression years, polenta was served at least three times a week, especially during the winter months, either at breakfast, or as a main course for lunch or dinner. Today, I serve it year-round in place of pasta, rice, bread, or potatoes.

When I first started teaching polenta courses during the seventies, the majority of my students had never heard of this dish. What truly amazed them was the variety of ways this cornmeal mush could be served. It can be topped with a sauce, made into a torte, canapés, baked as a pie, broiled, grilled, or sautéed for breakfast. Today, no matter in what part of the country I am teaching, more and more students are requesting variations on serving polenta.

I can still remember my first experience, at age twelve, cooking polenta under my mother's supervision. The cornmeal was first dissolved into a smooth creamy paste with a little water (so it produced fewer lumps). It was then slowly poured into her special large copper pot used exclusively for polenta called a paiolo, which contained boiling water or broth. The heat was turned down to low and she would hand me a long wooden spoon, also reserved for only making polenta. Then I was instructed to start the stirring process. "Follow the hand of the clock, Anna," she would repeat, insisting I stir and stir and stir in only one direction, for no less than 45 minutes. It was finally done when the polenta was smooth and thick and slowly fell off the lifted spoon, and the wooden spoon could stand up unsupported in the middle of the pan. In retrospect, I can't help but feel that most of this long cooking procedure was designed to keep me occupied while she prepared the rest of the meal.

After experimenting with a number of methods of cooking polenta, I have found absolutely no difference in texture in the finished dish, whether it is cooked for 20 to 25 minutes, or for Mama's mandatory 45! The two important lessons I did learn from Mama are that the polenta must be stirred constantly so that it will not produce lumps, and that it is done when it is smooth and thick and very slowly falls off the lifted spoon. I have also learned, many years later, that changing direction while stirring does not affect the quality of the finished product, that standing the wooden spoon in the middle of the pan is unnecessary, and that a heavy saucepan works just as well as her paiolo.

I have trial-tested many different brands of commercial yellow cornmeal and find that the medium-grained variety labeled "stone-ground" produces a wonderfully thick, smooth polenta. For recipes in this chapter, purchase either the yellow Indian Head stone-ground or Goya brands available in local supermarket or health food stores. If you prefer, you can also purchase coarse-grained varieties imported from Italy in either Italian specialty or gourmet shops. Both varieties work equally well. Cornmeal can be sealed and stored in the refrigerator up to 3 months, or in the freezer twice as long.

In addition to the recipes that follow in this chapter, polenta can be topped with any of the sauces in the pasta chapter.

Basic Recipe for Polenta

❖

6 CUPS COOKED POLENTA

This basic polenta recipe can also be made with all water. It will not taste quite as rich, but will be just as good.

2	cups stone-ground yellow cornmeal		preferably homemade (page 4), or low-sodium canned
2	cups cold water		
4	cups Vegetable Broth,	½	teaspoon coarse salt

1. Place cornmeal into a medium-size bowl. Add water and stir with whisk until you have a smooth creamy paste.
2. In a heavy 3½-quart saucepan, bring broth to a boil over high heat and add salt. Slowly pour in the cornmeal mixture, whisking constantly to prevent any lumps from forming. Turn heat to medium-low and simmer, stirring constantly with a long-handled wooden spoon to keep the mixture smooth. If some lumps form in cooking, push them against the sides of the pan with spoon to dissolve. Polenta will be done when the mixture is smooth and thick and very slowly falls off lifted spoon, about 20 to 25 minutes.

Per Cup: Cal. 151   Carb. 31 gm   Chol. 0 mg
          Fat 1 gm   Prot. 5 gm   Sod. 133 mg

Baked Layered Polenta Torte

[Torta di Polenta]

SERVES 6

An earthy, satisfying single-course dinner. Nothing more is needed than a tossed green salad. This dish can be completely assembled up to 5 hours before baking. Cover with plastic wrap and refrigerate. Remove from refrigerator 1 hour before baking.

1½ cups Tomato-Basil Sauce (page 24)
1 pound spinach
2 tablespoons fine dry bread crumbs
Basic Recipe for Polenta (page 54)

¼ cup grated pecorino romano cheese
2 tablespoons minced Italian flat leaf parsley, for garnish

1. Prepare tomato-basil sauce up to 3 hours before cooking polenta.
2. Trim stems from spinach and wash several times in tepid water. Place in 3½-quart saucepan. Do not add water; the final rinse water clinging to leaves will be sufficient to steam them. Cook, covered, over high heat until wilted, about 3 minutes. Thoroughly drain in colander. When cool enough to handle, thoroughly squeeze out excess moisture and chop fine; set aside.
3. Lightly grease bottom and sides of a 9-inch springform pan with olive oil cooking spray. Sprinkle bottom of pan with bread crumbs. Place pan on a large square of aluminum foil and wrap around bottom and halfway up sides of pan to prevent leakage while baking.
4. Make polenta. As soon as polenta is cooked, transfer 2 cups to a bowl and stir in spinach. Spoon half of the remaining polenta in bottom of prepared pan and spread evenly with a wet narrow metal spatula. Spread ½ cup sauce over polenta and sprinkle with 1 tablespoon cheese. Spread the spinach-polenta mixture atop. Spoon an-

other ½ cup sauce and 1 tablespoon cheese atop. Spread remaining polenta over top and spoon remaining ½ cup sauce over polenta. Sprinkle with remaining 2 tablespoons of cheese.

5. Adjust oven rack to middle of oven and preheat to 350° F. Bake torte until surface is crusty, about 50 minutes. Remove from oven, tent with foil, and let stand for at least 15 minutes before serving. Discard foil; run a knife around inside of pan and remove spring-form. Place torte on a flat plate with a folded piece of dampened paper towel in center to prevent bottom of pan from sliding when slicing. Garnish with minced parsley, slice into wedges, and serve.

Per Serving: Cal. 226   Carb. 40 gm   Chol. 3 mg
               Fat 5 gm   Prot. 8 gm   Sod. 423 mg

Breakfast Polenta

[Polenta di Colazione]

10 SLICES

Breakfast polenta can be made and stored in the refrigerator up to 4 days. Sautéed polenta may be topped with a little maple syrup or with berries, sliced fresh seasonal fruit, or unsweetened applesauce. If you like, drizzle a little honey over fruit.

2 cups stone-ground yellow cornmeal	5½ cups skim milk
	1 teaspoon coarse salt

1. Place cornmeal in a medium-size bowl. Add 2 cups milk and stir with whisk until you have a smooth creamy paste.
2. In heavy 3-quart saucepan, place remaining 3¼ cups milk, bring to a boil over medium-low heat, and add salt. Slowly pour in the corn-

meal mixture, whisking constantly to prevent any lumps from forming. Simmer, stirring constantly with a long-handled wooden spoon, to keep the mixture smooth. If some lumps form in cooking, push them against the sides of the pan with spoon to dissolve. Polenta will be done when the mixture is smooth, very thick, and slowly falls off lifted spoon, about 20 to 25 minutes.

3. Lightly spray bottom and sides of an 8½ × 4½ × 2½-inch glass loaf pan with cooking spray. Spoon polenta into pan and spread evenly with a wet narrow metal spatula. Cool to room temperature and cover with plastic wrap. Place in refrigerator and chill until firm, about 3 hours or overnight. Run a knife around inside edge of pan to loosen polenta; invert onto a board and slice into 10 even pieces; wipe knife with dampened cloth to prevent sticking while slicing. Place slices between layers of paper towel and blot out excess moisture. (Slices may be placed on platter in single layer, covered with plastic wrap, and refrigerated up to 4 days. Blot dry once again before sautéing.)

4. Spray a 10-inch nonstick skillet with cooking spray. Heat pan over medium-low heat. Place 2 slices of polenta in pan and sauté until lightly golden and crusty, about 2 to 3 minutes on each side. Transfer to plates and serve with any of the suggested toppings. (If sautéing more than 2 slices, wash and dry pan, respray, and repeat procedure.)

Per Slice: Cal. 126   Carb. 22 gm   Chol. 3 mg
              Fat 1 gm   Prot. 7 gm   Sod. 214 mg

Polenta Canapés

[Crostini di Polenta]

24 CANAPÉS

An excellent canapé to serve before dinner with a glass of chilled white wine. For ease in preparation, make the relish up to 2 days ahead and cook polenta 1 day in advance. This recipe differs slightly from the basic polenta recipe. The amount of liquid is reduced, producing a denser polenta that holds up well when broiled.

2¼ cups Sicilian Eggplant Relish (page 109)	½ cup minced Italian flat-leaf parsley
2 cups stone-ground yellow cornmeal	2 tablespoons olive oil
5¼ cups water	1 small bunch stemmed curly parsley, for garnish
½ teaspoon coarse salt	
½ teaspoon crushed red pepper flakes	

1. Prepare Sicilian eggplant relish up to 2 days ahead of cooking polenta. Reheat relish, covered, over low heat while broiling polenta.
2. Place cornmeal in a medium-size bowl. Add 2 cups water and stir with whisk until you have a smooth creamy paste.
3. In a heavy 3½-quart saucepan, bring remaining 3¼ cups water to a boil and add salt. Slowly pour in the cornmeal mixture, whisking constantly to prevent lumps from forming. Turn heat to medium-low and simmer, stirring constantly with a long-handled wooden spoon to keep the mixture smooth. If some lumps form in cooking, push them against the sides of the pan with spoon to dissolve. Polenta will be done when the mixture is smooth, very thick, and slowly falls off lifted spoon, about 20 to 25 minutes. Stir in pepper flakes and Italian parsley; remove from heat.
4. Lightly spray a 10½ × 15½-inch jelly roll pan with olive oil cook-

ing spray. Spoon polenta into prepared pan. Dip a narrow metal spatula in warm water and spread polenta evenly, dipping spatula several times in warm water to spread uniformly. Let cool to room temperature, cover with plastic wrap, and refrigerate until firm and well chilled, about 3 hours or overnight.

5. Adjust oven rack to 4 inches from broiler and preheat to broil setting. Lightly spray a 14 × 17-inch cookie sheet with olive oil cooking spray; set aside.

6. Run a knife around inside edge of pan to loosen polenta. Invert onto a large cutting board. Cut into 12 squares. Thoroughly blot dry between sheets of paper towel. Cut each square into 2 triangles. Place on prepared cookie sheet, spacing them ½ inch apart, and lightly brush surfaces with 1 tablespoon olive oil. Place in oven and broil until surfaces are golden brown, about 3 to 4 minutes. Remove from oven and turn triangles over. Brush with remaining 1 tablespoon olive oil, return to oven, and broil until second side is golden brown. Transfer to platter, spread 1½ tablespoons warmed relish over each, garnish with curly parsley, and serve.

| Per Canapé: | Cal. 38 | Carb. 7 gm | Chol. 0 mg |
| | Fat 1 gm | Prot. 1 gm | Sod. 65 mg |

Polenta with Eggplant and Roasted Pepper Sauce

[Polenta con Salsa di Melanzane e Peperoncini Arostiti]

SERVES 6

If you don't have time to roast peppers, substitute two 7-ounce jars of roasted peppers, rinsed and well drained before slicing.

1 large firm purple eggplant (about 1½ pounds), washed, ends trimmed, peeled, and cut into ½-inch cubes

1½ tablespoons coarse salt

1 tablespoon extra virgin olive oil

1 cup thinly sliced scallions

2 teaspoons minced garlic

8 medium well-ripened plum tomatoes (about 1 pound), blanched and peeled (see page 126 for technique), coarsely chopped, with juice included

2 tablespoons minced fresh basil or 2 teaspoons dried basil

½ teaspoon sugar

½ teaspoon freshly milled black pepper

3 large bell peppers (1½ pounds), roasted and peeled (see page 125 for technique), sliced lengthwise into ½-inch strips

Basic Recipe for Polenta (page 54)

3 tablespoons freshly grated imported Parmesan cheese

3 tablespoons minced Italian flat-leaf parsley, for garnish

1. Place diced eggplant in colander set over a shallow bowl. Sprinkle with salt and toss to combine. Place an inverted plate on top of eggplant; weight and drain for 30 minutes (a 28-ounce can of tomatoes works well for weighting). Thoroughly rinse eggplant in colander under cold running water. Take half of the eggplant and squeeze with your hands to get rid of some of the moisture. Place on kitchen towel and twist towel to squeeze out all of the moisture. Place in bowl and repeat with remaining eggplant.

2. In 12-inch nonstick skillet, heat olive oil over medium heat. Add scallions and sauté, stirring constantly, until tender, about 1 minute. Add garlic and cook, stirring constantly, until softened but not brown, about 1 minute. Add eggplant and sauté, stirring constantly, until barely tender-crisp, about 2 minutes. Stir in tomatoes, basil, sugar, and pepper. Cook, partially covered, stirring frequently, for 10 minutes. Add roasted peppers and continue to cook, uncovered, stirring frequently, until sauce is slightly thickened, about 10 minutes. (Sauce can be prepared up to 3 hours before cooking polenta. Reheat, covered, over low heat while cooking polenta.)

3. Make polenta. As soon as polenta is cooked, spoon onto a large platter. With the back of the spoon, spread polenta evenly to a thickness
   of about 1½ inches. Spoon sauce over polenta, leaving a 1-inch
   border of polenta showing on all sides. Sprinkle cheese over top,
   garnish with parsley, and serve.

Per Serving: Cal. 240   Carb. 48 gm   Chol. 2 mg
              Fat 5 gm   Prot. 8 gm   Sod. 286 mg

Polenta with Escarole and Kidney Beans

[Polenta alla Toscana]

SERVES 6

*This robust polenta dish is a favorite with students and family. It is on my
menu quite often during the winter months.*

Escarole and Kidney Beans   9   teaspoons grated pecorino
(page 112)   romano cheese
Basic Recipe for Polenta
(page 54)

1. Prepare the braised escarole and beans up to 3 hours before cooking polenta. Reheat over low heat while cooking polenta.
2. Make polenta. As soon as polenta is cooked, ladle into 6 soup
   plates. Spoon escarole and beans over polenta. Sprinkle 1½ teaspoons pecorino romano cheese over each dish and serve.

Per Serving: Cal. 265   Carb. 46 gm   Chol. 2 mg
              Fat 5 gm   Prot. 11 gm   Sod. 411 mg

Polenta with Leeks and Sage

[Polenta alla Lipani]

SERVES 6

This rustic one-dish meal was developed by my niece, Kristin Lipani, who loves making polenta and learned from her grandmother, who came from the Piedmont region of Italy. Serve with Zucchini and Roasted Pepper Salad (page 151).

1 tablespoon olive oil	½ teaspoon coarse salt
3 large leeks (about 1 pound), roots and tops trimmed, split in half lengthwise, thoroughly washed, and thinly sliced to make 4 cups, well packed	½ teaspoon freshly milled white pepper
	Basic Recipe for Polenta (page 54)
¾ cup dry white wine	3 tablespoons freshly grated Parmesan cheese
1 tablespoon minced fresh sage or 1 teaspoon crumbled dried sage	4 sprigs fresh sage, for garnish

1. In a 12-inch nonstick skillet, heat olive oil over low heat. Add leeks and cook until lightly golden, about 4 minutes. If leeks start to stick to bottom of pan, loosen with 2 tablespoons wine. Add wine and continue to cook, stirring frequently, until leeks are tender, about 12 to 15 minutes. Turn heat to medium-high, add sage, and cook, stirring frequently, until very little liquid is left in bottom of pan, about 2 minutes. Season with salt and pepper; remove from heat. (Leeks can be cooked up to 2 hours before cooking polenta. Reheat, covered, over low heat while cooking polenta.)

2. Make polenta. As soon as polenta is cooked, spoon onto a large platter. With the back of the spoon, spread polenta evenly to a thickness of about 1½ inches. Spoon cooked leeks over polenta, leaving a

1-inch border of polenta showing on all sides. Sprinkle cheese over top, garnish with sage sprigs, and serve.

Per Serving: Cal. 202   Carb. 36 gm   Chol. 2 mg
               Fat 4 gm   Prot. 6 gm   Sod. 276 mg

Polenta Pie with Mushroom Filling
[Torta di Polenta alla Genovese]

SERVES 6

This hearty Ligurian pie was once considered peasant fare. Not so any longer! Soothing comfort food like this is now appreciated for its simple goodness. All that is needed to complete this meal is the Broccoli Salad with Lemon-Honey Dressing (page 140)

½   ounce dried Italian porcini mushrooms
1½ tablespoons tomato paste
1   tablespoon olive oil
⅓   cup minced red onion
2   teaspoons minced garlic
12 ounces white mushrooms, stemmed, wiped, and thinly sliced

½   cup dry red wine
1½ teaspoons minced fresh rosemary or ¼ teaspoon chopped dried rosemary
½   teaspoon freshly milled black pepper
    Basic Recipe for Polenta (page 54)
1   egg white, lightly beaten

1. Soak dried mushrooms in 1 cup warm water for 30 minutes. Drain mushrooms in a strainer, reserving liquid. Rinse mushrooms in cold

〰〰

water, blot dry, finely chop, and set aside. Pour reserved liquid through strainer lined with paper towel set over a small bowl to remove sand. Add tomato paste to strained liquid and stir to dissolve; set aside.

2. In a 12-inch nonstick skillet, heat olive oil over medium-low heat. Add onion and cook until barely tender, about 2 minutes. Add garlic and cook for an additional 30 seconds. Stir in white mushrooms and sauté until barely tender, about 2 minutes. Stir in wine and dried mushrooms, raise heat to medium-high, and cook until liquid in pan is reduced to about 2 tablespoons, about 2 minutes. Stir in the dissolved tomato paste mixture; cook, stirring frequently, until there is no liquid left in pan and mixture is a smooth thick paste, about 5 minutes. Stir in rosemary, season with pepper, and remove from heat. Filling can be made up to 3 hours before cooking polenta.

3. Lightly grease bottom and sides of a 10-inch pie pan with olive oil cooking spray; set aside.

4. Make polenta. As soon as polenta is cooked, spoon half into prepared pan and spread evenly with back of spoon. Spoon mushroom filling on top and spread evenly to within ½ inch of outside rim of polenta. Brush rim of polenta with lightly beaten egg white. Reserve remaining egg white. Carefully spoon remaining polenta over filling. Dip a narrow metal spatula in warm water and spread polenta evenly, dipping spatula 2 or 3 more times in warm water to spread top crust uniformly. (Pie can be assembled up to 3 hours before baking. Cool to room temperature, cover with plastic wrap, and set aside until ready to bake.)

5. Adjust oven rack to center of oven and preheat to 375° F.

6. Remove plastic wrap and brush entire surface of pie with lightly beaten egg white. Bake in preheated oven until surface is crusty and lightly browned, about 50 to 55 minutes. Remove from oven and let rest for at least 15 minutes before serving. Slice into wedges like a pie and serve.

Per Serving: Cal. 200   Carb. 36 gm   Chol. 0 mg
              Fat 4 gm   Prot. 6 gm   Sod. 179 mg

Polenta with Sun-Dried Tomatoes and Basil

[Polenta Arrostita]

8 SLICES

This recipe differs slightly from the basic polenta recipe. The amount of liquid is reduced, producing a denser polenta that holds up well when broiled or grilled. The polenta can be made 2 days in advance, covered with plastic wrap, and refrigerated until needed. This polenta dish may be served in place of bread, pasta, or rice.

½ cup well-packed sun-dried tomatoes, not packed in oil

2 cups stone-ground yellow cornmeal

5¼ cups water

½ teaspoon coarse salt

½ teaspoon freshly milled white pepper

3 tablespoons minced fresh basil

4 teaspoons extra virgin olive oil

8 sprigs fresh basil, for garnish

1. Place sun-dried tomatoes in a bowl and pour on boiling water to cover. Let stand 2 minutes to soften; drain thoroughly. When cool enough to handle, finely chop tomatoes and set aside.
2. Place cornmeal in a medium-size bowl. Add 2 cups water and stir with whisk until you have a smooth creamy paste.
3. In a heavy 3½-quart saucepan, bring remaining 3¼ cups water to a boil over high heat and add salt. Slowly pour in the cornmeal mixture, whisking constantly to prevent any lumps from forming. Turn heat to low and simmer, stirring frequently with a long-handled wooden spoon, to keep the mixture smooth. If some lumps form in cooking, push them against the sides of the pan with spoon to dis-

solve. Polenta will be done when the mixture is smooth, very thick, and slowly falls off lifted spoon, about 20 to 25 minutes. Stir in sun-dried tomatoes, pepper, and basil; remove from heat.

4. Lightly spray a 9 × 13 × 2-inch baking dish with olive oil cooking spray. Spoon polenta into prepared dish. Dip a narrow metal spatula in warm water and spread polenta evenly, dipping spatula several times in warm water to spread uniformly. Cool to room temperature, cover with plastic wrap, and refrigerate until firm and well chilled, at least 4 hours or up to 2 days.

5. Adjust oven rack to 4 inches from heat source and preheat to broil setting. Grease surface of broiler rack set over broiler pan with olive oil cooking spray.

6. Run a knife around inside edge of baking dish to loosen polenta. Invert onto a board. Slice into 8 even pieces. Thoroughly blot dry between sheets of paper towel.

7. Place on broiler rack and brush each slice with ¼ teaspoon olive oil. Place in oven and broil until golden brown, about 5 to 6 minutes. Remove from oven and turn slices over. Brush with remaining oil, return to oven, and broil until second side is golden brown. Transfer to platter, garnish with basil, and serve.

Per Slice:	Cal. 135	Carb. 24 gm	Chol. 0 mg
	Fat 3 gm	Prot. 4 gm	Sod. 97 mg

Rice

Introduction

Rice, pasta, and polenta are conceivably the most versatile and variable foods in the Italian diet. Rice can provide the basis of any meal and be used with equal success in any dish—soup, salad, risotto, entrée accompaniment, or dessert.

In this chapter three different types of rice are used. The long-grain is excellent for general use in baked rice, combined with vegetables, topped off with a tomato sauce, or in a salad. The brown rice with its nutty flavor goes extremely well with fennel as a side dish. It can also be interchanged with any of the above dishes, but follow package directions for extended cooking time. For risotto, I am a purist and insist that the short-grain Italian rice, arborio, is the prime choice. Do not be tempted by round rice or any other short-grain. Though similar in appearance to Italian short-grain rice, they do not have the starch that simultaneously acts to thicken the dish and promote a high absorption of the wine and broth used to cook it. The most popular variety of Italian short-grain rice is labeled "arborio" and comes from the Piedmont section of Italy. Arborio is available in many supermarkets, gourmet shops, and Italian specialty stores. Several other varieties of the same type are beginning to appear in Italian specialty stores as well. The two most popular brands are Vialone Nano and Carnaroli.

Risotto is that magical mixture of rice cooked to a creamy perfection in wine and broth, after which it can be beautifully blended with a variety of vegetables. The following are a few helpful hints for cooking perfect risotto:

- Prepare all of your ingredients in advance and line them up in bowls.
- Do not rinse the rice. Rinsing causes premature starch release.
- Use a heavy saucepan with a flat bottom and straight sides to ensure even cooking.
- Never let the vegetable broth get cold. Keep it simmering in a separate saucepan. The temperature of the dish must remain constant to prevent stickiness. Slow addition of hot broth is mandatory.
- The most import stage of cooking risotto is the last few minutes. At that point add very little broth. It is easier to add broth if needed than to have a risotto of a soupy consistency.
- The rice keeps cooking even after it is removed from the heat, and

tends to dry out fast. Be sure your guests or family are seated at the table before serving, so that the rice is still gently firm to the bite and moist and creamy when served.

In addition to the rice recipes in this chapter, there is a Creamy Rice Pudding (page 192) in the chapter on desserts.

Asparagus and Yellow Pepper Risotto

[Risotto Primavera]

SERVES 4

Select medium-size asparagus spears to ensure even cooking. This is a taste-enlivening dish to serve during the spring season when asparagus is moderately priced at the market. Serve this entrée with Mixed Green Salad with Fresh Tomato-Herb Dressing (page 142).

1¼ pounds medium-size asparagus	strings removed before chopping
5 to 5½ cups Vegetable Broth, preferably homemade (page 4), or low-sodium canned	½ cup dry white wine
	1⅓ cups arborio rice, picked over to remove any dark grains
1 large firm yellow bell pepper (8 ounces), halved, cored, seeded, deribbed, and cut into 1-inch-long strips	¼ teaspoon coarse salt
	¼ teaspoon freshly milled black pepper
	¼ cup snipped fresh chives, for garnish
2 teaspoons olive oil	8 teaspoons freshly grated mellow Asiago cheese
⅓ cup minced onion	
¼ cup finely chopped celery,	

1. Wash asparagus several times in cold water to remove sand. Using a sharp knife, cut off woody ends at base of spears. With a vegetable peeler, peel stalks from the base of the spear up, leaving tips intact. Slice stalks diagonally into 1-inch lengths; reserve tips.
2. In a 4-quart saucepan, bring broth to a boil over medium high heat. Add sliced asparagus stalks and cook until barely tender, about

2 minutes. Add the asparagus tips and bell pepper; continue cooking until tender, about 2 to 3 minutes. Using a slotted spoon, transfer vegetables to a bowl. Keep broth at a bare simmer over low heat.

3. In a heavy 5-quart saucepan, heat olive oil over medium-low heat. Add onion and celery. Sauté, stirring constantly with wooden spoon, until tender-crisp, about 2 minutes. (If vegetables start to stick to bottom of pan, add 2 tablespoons broth to prevent scorching.) Add the rice and ½ cup broth. Cook, stirring constantly, until rice is opaque and well coated. Add the wine and cook mixture, stirring constantly, until all the wine has been absorbed, about 1 minute. Add 1 cup broth and cook, stirring constantly, until all the liquid has been absorbed. Watch carefully so the rice does not stick to bottom of pan. Add more broth, 1 cup at a time, stirring constantly and cooking the mixture until all the liquid is absorbed after each addition. After 5 cups of broth have been added, the rice should be tender and have a creamy consistency. Test by tasting a few grains; it should be soft on the outside and a bit chewy on the inside. If necessary, add the remaining ½ cup broth and cook in the same manner until rice is tender. Total cooking time will be approximately 20 to 25 minutes. Stir in the asparagus and pepper strips; simmer the risotto, stirring constantly, until the vegetables are heated through, about 30 seconds. Remove from heat, transfer to individual bowls, and garnish each with 1 tablespoon snipped chives. Serve with Asiago cheese.

Per Serving: Cal. 378   Carb. 70 gm   Chol. 3 mg
              Fat 4 gm   Prot. 11 gm   Sod. 178 mg

Baked Rice with Ricotta

[Riso con Ricotta al Forno]

❖

SERVES 8

This rice is more like a baked custard: crusty on top and moist in the center. Perfect partners are Sautéed Mushrooms with Sun-dried Tomatoes (page 117) and the Vegetable Medley with Balsamic Dressing (page 149).

1½ cups arborio or long-grain rice, picked over to remove any dark grains
½ cup fat-free egg substitute
1¾ cups skim milk
¼ cup freshly grated imported Parmesan cheese

1 cup part-skim ricotta cheese
¼ cup finely minced Italian flat-leaf parsley
½ teaspoon coarse salt
¼ teaspoon freshly milled white pepper

1. Cook rice in 4 quarts boiling water until barely tender, about 7 minutes. Transfer to a fine mesh strainer and cool to room temperature.
2. Adjust oven rack one-third up from bottom of oven and preheat to 350°F. Lightly grease a 9 × 13 × 2-inch ovenproof baking dish with olive oil cooking spray.
3. In a deep bowl, whisk together egg substitute and milk. Add the Parmesan cheese, ricotta, parsley, salt, and pepper; whisk until blended. Stir in rice and mix well. Pour into prepared pan. Cover with a piece of parchment paper that has been lightly sprayed with olive oil cooking spray. Cover pan with aluminum foil. Bake in preheated oven until a knife inserted in center comes out clean, about 40 to 45 minutes. Remove from oven; discard foil and parchment paper.
4. Adjust oven rack 4 inches from heat source and preheat to broil setting.

5. Return rice to oven and broil until surface is lightly golden, about 2 to 3 minutes. Transfer to cooling rack and let rest for 10 minutes before slicing into squares to serve.

Per Serving: Cal. 212   Carb. 34 gm   Chol. 12 mg
              Fat 3 gm   Prot. 10 gm   Sod. 196 mg

Broccoli and Lemon Risotto

[Risotto con Broccoli e Limone]

SERVES 6

The grated lemon zest and fresh lemon juice add a piquant flavor to this risotto. The Zucchini and Roasted Pepper Salad (page 151) with some crusty Italian bread will round out this meal.

1 large bunch broccoli (about 1½ pounds)

6½ to 7 cups Vegetable Broth, preferably homemade (page 4), or low-sodium canned

1 tablespoon finely grated lemon zest

2 tablespoons strained fresh lemon juice

1 tablespoon olive oil

1 medium leek (about 4 ounces), split in half lengthwise, thoroughly washed, and thinly sliced to make 1 cup

2 cups arborio rice, picked over to remove any dark grains

1 cup dry white wine

½ teaspoon coarse salt

¼ teaspoon freshly milled white pepper

¼ cup minced Italian flat-leaf parsley

〰〰

1. Remove florets from broccoli, leaving about ½ inch of stems. Cut florets into 1-inch pieces; wash in cold water, drain, and set aside. Remove and discard the large coarse leaves from stems; cut off about 1 inch of the tough lower part. Wash and peel stems with vegetable peeler; cut into ½-inch dice.

2. In a 4-quart saucepan, bring the broth to a boil over medium heat. Add florets and cook until barely tender, about 2 minutes. With a skimmer or slotted spoon, transfer florets to bowl and set aside. Add the lemon zest and juice to broth; keep at a simmer over low heat.

3. In a heavy 5-quart saucepan, heat olive oil over medium-low heat. Add leek and broccoli stems. Sauté, stirring frequently with a wooden spoon, until stems are barely tender, about 3 minutes. (If vegetables start to stick to bottom of pan, loosen with 2 table-spoons broth to prevent scorching.) Add the rice and ½ cup broth. Cook, stirring constantly, until rice is opaque and well coated. Add the wine and cook mixture, stirring constantly, until all the wine has been absorbed, about 2 minutes. Add 1½ cups broth and cook, stirring constantly, until all the liquid has been absorbed. Watch carefully so the rice does not stick to bottom of pan. Add more broth, 1 cup at a time, stirring constantly and cooking the mixture until all the liquid is absorbed after each addition. After 6½ cups of broth have been added, the rice should be tender and have a creamy consistency. Test by tasting a few grains; rice should be soft on the outside and a bit chewy on the inside. If necessary, add the remaining ½ cup broth and cook in the same manner until rice is tender. Total cooking time will be approximately 25 to 30 minutes. Stir in broccoli florets and simmer the risotto, stirring constantly, until florets are heated through, about 30 seconds. Season with salt and pepper; remove from heat. Stir in minced parsley, transfer to individual bowls, and serve.

Per Serving: Cal. 326   Carb. 67 gm   Chol. 0 mg
                Fat 3 gm   Prot. 8 gm   Sod. 169 mg

Brown Rice with Fennel

[Riso Scuro con Finocchio]

SERVES 4

This is a good dish to make in late fall or during the winter when large fennel bulbs are plentiful. Serve this rice dish with Braised Broccoli di Rape with Prunes (page 103) and Baby Spinach, Walnut, and Goat Cheese Salad (page 147).

1 large fennel bulb with leaves (about 1 pound), weighed with 2 inches of leaves

2 teaspoons olive oil

⅓ cup chopped shallots

1 cup long-grain brown rice, picked over to remove any dark brown grains

3 cups Vegetable Broth, preferably homemade (page 4), or low-sodium canned

½ teaspoon coarse salt

¼ teaspoon freshly milled black pepper

1. Remove small feathery leaves from top of fennel stalk; finely chop and reserve ¼ cup for garnish. Cut off upper stalks of bulb and discard. Trim base of bulbs. With a vegetable peeler, lightly peel outside of bulb to remove strings. Slice bulb in half vertically and remove center core with a V cut. Cut into ½-inch dice; set aside.

2. In a heavy 5-quart saucepan, heat olive oil over low heat. Add shallots and cook until soft but not brown, about 2 minutes. Stir in rice, fennel, and broth. Turn heat to high. As soon as broth comes to a boil, cover pan, turn heat to low, and simmer until rice is tender and all the liquid is absorbed, about 45 to 50 minutes. Remove from heat and season with salt and pepper. Transfer to bowl, garnish with chopped fennel leaves, and serve.

Per Serving: Cal. 232   Carb. 44 gm   Chol. 0 mg
             Fat 4 gm   Prot. 6 gm   Sod. 184 mg

Rice with Fresh Herbs

[Riso con Erbe Aromatiche]

❖

SERVES 6

This is one of my favorite rice dishes to make during the summer months when my herb garden is bursting with lush leafy basil, mint, parsley, and thyme.

2 teaspoons olive oil
¼ cup finely chopped onion
2 teaspoons minced garlic
1½ cups arborio or long-grain rice, picked over to remove any dark grains
4½ cups Vegetable Broth, preferably homemade (page 4), or low-sodium canned
½ teaspoon coarse salt

½ teaspoon crushed red pepper flakes
⅓ cup loosely packed snipped fresh basil leaves
¼ cup loosely packed snipped fresh mint leaves
¼ cup loosely packed minced Italian flat-leaf parsley
1 tablespoon minced fresh thyme

In a heavy 5-quart saucepan, heat olive oil over medium-low heat. Add onion and garlic and cook until soft but not brown, about 2 minutes. (If vegetables start to stick to bottom of pan, loosen with 2 tablespoons broth to prevent scorching.) Add rice and stir constantly until opaque and well coated. Add broth and turn heat to high. As soon as broth comes to a boil, cover pan, turn heat to low, and simmer until rice is tender, about 20 minutes. Season with salt and pepper flakes; remove from heat. Stir in all the fresh herbs, transfer to bowl, and serve.

Per Serving: Cal. 222   Carb. 46 gm   Chol. 0 mg
              Fat 2 gm   Prot. 4 gm   Sod. 137 mg

Rice with Mushrooms and Parsley

[Riso con Funghi]

SERVES 6

This rice dish is an excellent plate mate with Braised Romaine Lettuce (page 121) and Yellow Wax Beans with Olives and Sage (page 130).

3 cups water
1½ cups long-grain white rice, preferably Carolina, picked over to remove any dark grains
2 teaspoons olive oil
2 teaspoons minced garlic
8 ounces crimini or white mushrooms, stemmed, wiped, and thinly sliced
½ teaspoon coarse salt
½ teaspoon freshly milled black pepper
¼ cup minced Italian flat-leaf parsley

1. In a heavy 3-quart saucepan, bring water to a boil over high heat. Stir in rice, cover pan, reduce heat to low, and simmer until tender, about 15 to 18 minutes. Let stand, covered, for 5 minutes.
2. While rice is cooking, heat olive oil in a 10-inch nonstick skillet over medium-low heat. Add garlic and cook, stirring constantly, until lightly golden, about 30 seconds. Stir in mushrooms and cook, stirring frequently, until tender, about 2 minutes. Remove from heat and season with salt and pepper.
3. Fluff rice a few times with two forks. Transfer to bowl and stir in mushroom mixture and parsley. Serve immediately.

Per Serving: Cal. 192   Carb. 39 gm   Chol. 0 mg
Fat 2 gm   Prot. 4 gm   Sod. 127 mg

Rice with Tomato-Basil Sauce

[Riso con Salsa di Pomodoro]

SERVES 4

This rice dish is ready in a matter of minutes if you have some tomato-basil sauce on hand. A good accompaniment to Dandelion Greens with Crispy Garlic (page 107) and Simple Green Beans (page 113).

1 cup Tomato-Basil Sauce (page 24)	¼ teaspoon freshly milled black pepper
1 cup arborio or long-grain rice, picked over to remove any dark grains	1½ tablespoons freshly grated imported Parmesan cheese
½ teaspoon coarse salt	1 tablespoon minced Italian flat-leaf parsley

1. Prepare sauce 2 hours before cooking rice.
2. In a heavy 5-quart pot, bring 3 quarts water to a rolling boil over high heat. Add rice and stir once with wooden spoon so the rice does not stick to the bottom of pot. When water returns to a boil, reduce heat and simmer, uncovered, until rice is tender, about 12 to 15 minutes. Drain in a fine mesh strainer and transfer to a deep bowl.
3. While rice is cooking, heat sauce over low heat. Stir sauce into cooked rice; season with salt and pepper. Stir in cheese and parsley, transfer to bowl, and serve.

Per Serving: Cal. 223   Carb. 45 gm   Chol. 1 mg
              Fat 2 gm   Prot. 4 gm   Sod. 360 mg

Rice and Double Bean Salad

[Insalata di Riso]

SERVES 8

A dazzling salad to bring to a covered dish supper, picnic, or tailgate party.

1¼ pounds green beans, trimmed and washed	2 teaspoons minced fresh thyme or ½ teaspoon dried thyme
1½ cups arborio or long-grain rice, picked over to remove any dark grains	½ teaspoon coarse salt
4 medium well-ripened plum tomatoes (about 8 ounces), halved, cored, and finely chopped	½ teaspoon freshly milled black pepper
½ cup thinly sliced scallions	2 tablespoons white wine vinegar
1 can (15 ounces) dark red kidney beans, rinsed and thoroughly drained	½ teaspoon Dijon-style mustard
1 teaspoon minced fresh oregano or ¼ teaspoon dried oregano	¼ teaspoon sugar
	1½ tablespoons extra virgin olive oil

1. Put green beans in a steamer with 1 inch of water in bottom of 4-quart saucepan. Cook, covered, over medium-high heat until tender, about 4 minutes. Remove steamer and let beans cool to room temperature. When cool enough to handle, cut beans diagonally

into 1-inch lengths; set aside. Measure out ⅓ cup liquid from bottom of saucepan and reserve for dressing.

2. While green beans are cooking, bring 4 quarts of water to a rolling boil in a 6-quart pot over high heat. Add rice and stir once with wooden spoon so the rice does not stick to bottom of pot. When water returns to a boil, reduce the heat to medium and cook, uncovered, until tender, about 15 to 20 minutes. Drain in strainer and refresh under cold water. Drain again and transfer to a deep bowl. Cool rice to room temperature. Add green beans, tomatoes, scallions, kidney beans, oregano, and thyme; toss gently to combine.

3. In a small bowl, combine reserved ⅓ cup cooking liquid with salt, pepper, vinegar, mustard, and sugar; stir with fork or small whisk to combine. Add olive oil and whisk until dressing is well blended. Pour dressing over salad and gently mix with 2 forks. (Salad can be prepared up to 3 hours before serving. Cover with plastic wrap and leave at room temperature. Toss once again before serving.)

Per Serving: Cal. 221   Carb. 42 gm   Chol. 0 mg
               Fat 3 gm   Prot. 7 gm   Sod. 173 mg

Sun-Dried Tomato Risotto

[Risotto con Pomodoro Secco]

SERVES 4

All that is needed to complete this Ligurian entrée is the Arugula, Mushroom, and Radish Salad (page 136).

½ cup well-packed sun-dried tomatoes, not packed in oil

1¼ cups water

4½ cups Vegetable Broth, preferably homemade (page 4), or low-sodium canned

2 teaspoons olive oil

½ cup thinly sliced scallions (white part and 2 inches of the green)

2 teaspoons minced garlic

1⅓ cups arborio rice, picked over to remove any dark grains

½ cup dry white wine

2 teaspoons minced fresh thyme or ½ teaspoon dried thyme

¼ teaspoon coarse salt

¼ teaspoon freshly milled white pepper

¼ cup snipped green tops of scallions, for garnish

8 teaspoons freshly grated Parmesan cheese

1. Place sun-dried tomatoes and water in a 1-quart saucepan. Bring to a boil over low heat. Remove from heat and let stand until tomatoes are soft, about 3 minutes. Drain in strainer set over a bowl, reserving 1 cup liquid. When tomatoes are cool enough to handle, slice diagonally into ½-inch strips; set aside.

2. In a 2½-quart saucepan, combine the reserved tomato liquid and the broth. Heat over low heat and keep the broth mixture at a bare simmer over low heat.

3. In a heavy 5-quart saucepan, heat olive oil over medium-low heat. Add scallions and garlic; cook, stirring frequently with wooden spoon, until barely tender, about 1 minute. Add the rice and ½ cup of the broth mixture. Cook, stirring constantly, until rice is opaque and well coated. Add the wine and cook mixture, stirring constantly, until all the wine has been absorbed, about 2 minutes. Add the sun-dried tomatoes, thyme, and 1 cup broth mixture to the rice. Cook, stirring constantly, until all the liquid has been absorbed. Watch carefully so the rice does not stick to bottom of pan. Add more broth mixture, 1 cup at a time, stirring constantly, and cooking mixture until all the liquid is absorbed after each addition. After 5 cups of broth mixture have been added, the rice should be tender and have a creamy consistency. Test by tasting a few grains; it should be soft on the outside and just a bit chewy on the inside. If necessary, add the remaining ½ cup broth mixture and continue

cooking rice in the same manner until tender. Total cooking time will be approximately 20 to 25 minutes. Remove pan from heat; season with salt and pepper. Transfer to platter and garnish with snipped scallions. Serve with Parmesan cheese.

Per Serving: Cal. 350   Carb. 66 gm   Chol. 3 mg
              Fat 4 gm   Prot. 8 gm   Sod. 143 mg

Tomato and Zucchini Risotto

[Risotto alla Stabiano]

SERVES 6

An excellent accompaniment to this distinguished Tuscan-style risotto would be the Grilled Portobello Mushrooms with Lemon Dressing (page 115).

1 tablespoon olive oil
½ cup chopped red onion
8 large well-ripened plum tomatoes (about 1½ pounds), blanched and peeled (see page 124 for technique), coarsely chopped, with juice included
½ teaspoon coarse salt
½ teaspoon freshly milled black pepper
¼ teaspoon sugar
2 tablespoons minced fresh basil or 2 teaspoons dried basil

5 to 5½ cups Vegetable Broth, preferably homemade (page 4), or low-sodium canned
2 cups arborio rice, picked over to remove any dark grains
½ cup dry vermouth
3 small zucchini (about 1 pound), scrubbed, trimmed, and cut into strips 1 inch long by ¼ inch wide
2 tablespoons minced Italian flat-leaf parsley, for garnish

1. In a heavy 5-quart saucepan, heat olive oil over low heat. Add onion and cook, stirring frequently, until soft, about 3 minutes. Stir in tomatoes, salt, pepper, sugar, and basil. Turn heat to medium-high and bring to a boil. Cook, stirring frequently, until sauce is slightly thickened, about 10 minutes.
2. While sauce is cooking, heat broth in a 2½-quart saucepan over low heat. Keep the broth at a simmer over low heat.
3. Add rice to sauce, turn heat to medium, and cook, stirring constantly with wooden spoon, until rice is well coated. Add the vermouth and cook mixture, stirring constantly, until all the liquid has been absorbed, about 1 minute. Add 1½ cups broth to the rice and cook over medium-low heat, stirring constantly, until all the liquid has been absorbed. Watch carefully so the rice does not stick to bottom of pan. Add more broth, 1 cup at a time, stirring frequently and cooking the mixture until all the liquid is absorbed after each addition. After 4 cups of broth have been added, the rice should be barely tender. Stir in the zucchini and another 1 cup of the broth. Turn heat to low and simmer the mixture, stirring constantly, until the zucchini are tender and all the liquid is absorbed, about 3 to 4 minutes. When finished, the rice should be tender and have a creamy consistency. Test by tasting a few grains; rice should be soft on the outside and a bit chewy on the inside. If necessary, add the remaining ½ cup broth to the rice and continue to cook in the same manner until tender. Total cooking time will be approximately 25 to 30 minutes. Remove from heat and transfer to individual bowls. Garnish each with 1 teaspoon minced parsley and serve.

Per Serving:	Cal. 333	Carb. 70 gm	Chol. 0 mg
	Fat 3 gm	Prot. 7 gm	Sod. 153 mg

Vegetable Entrées and Vegetable Side Dishes

Introduction

Vegetable Entrées

EGGPLANT ROLLS WITH TOMATO-BASIL SAUCE

FENNEL STEW WITH CARROTS AND POTATOES

GREEN PEPPERS STUFFED WITH ORZO

STUFFED SUMMER SQUASH WITH COUSCOUS

TUSCAN TOMATO AND BEAN STEW WITH SAGE

VEGGIE BURGERS WITH TOMATO-THYME SAUCE

SUMMER GARDEN STEW

WINTER VEGETABLE STEW

Vegetable Side Dishes

STUFFED ARTICHOKES WITH SUN-DRIED TOMATOES AND HERBS

ASPARAGUS WITH LEMON AND THYME

BRAISED BROCCOLI DI RAPE WITH PRUNES

BRUSSELS SPROUTS WITH HERBED BREAD CRUMBS

BUTTERNUT SQUASH WITH SAGE

DANDELION GREENS WITH CRISPY GARLIC

SICILIAN EGGPLANT RELISH

BRAISED BELGIAN ENDIVE

ESCAROLE AND KIDNEY BEANS

SIMPLE GREEN BEANS

KALE WITH RAISINS AND PINE NUTS

GRILLED PORTOBELLO MUSHROOMS WITH LEMON DRESSING

SAUTÉED MUSHROOMS WITH SUN-DRIED TOMATOES

STUFFED BAKED POTATOES WITH SUN-DRIED TOMATOES
AND DILL

MASHED POTATOES WITH GARLIC AND ROSEMARY

BRAISED ROMAINE LETTUCE

WILTED SPINACH WITH GARLIC

SWISS CHARD WITH BALSAMIC VINEGAR

TECHNIQUE FOR ROASTING PEPPERS

TECHNIQUE FOR BLANCHING TOMATOES

SICILIAN-STYLE BAKED TURNIPS

GRILLED WHITE EGGPLANT

YELLOW WAX BEANS WITH OLIVES AND SAGE

When it comes to selecting vegetables either at the produce section of the supermarket or at the local open-air or farmers' markets, I'm like a kid let loose in a candy store. I scan the produce displays, inspecting each with a critical eye for the freshest seasonal varieties available. As a child, I would pull my wagon and follow my mother to the vegetable market and watch her examine every vegetable and fruit before making her choices. She would snap the green beans for tenderness, turn the broccoli over to make sure no yellow spots prevailed, hand-pick each eggplant for firmness, inspect each mushroom to make sure no gills were showing, and practically interview each plum or round tomato before finally making her selections. She was a true vegetarian in the sense that she rarely ate meat but would prepare at least three different vegetables for lunch or dinner and combine them with pasta, rice, or polenta to create unusual meatless entrées. Each season brought with it an exciting, distinct, vegetable stew we called ciambotta. While a garden stew of zucchini, tomato, and eggplant signaled summer, cauliflower, broccoli, and carrots heralded fall and winter, and green beans, asparagus, and new potatoes sang of spring. Vegetables varied according to the season or the mood of the cook.

In many cuisines, vegetables are afterthoughts. But when Italian cooks take to steaming, sautéing, braising, baking, or grilling their vegetables, their results are full of imagination and flavor. Recipes such as Braised Broccoli di Rape with Prunes, Butternut Squash with Sage, Mashed Potatoes with Garlic and Rosemary, Grilled Portobello Mushrooms with Lemon Dressing, and Swiss Chard with Balsamic Vinegar move vegetables from the wings to center stage.

The recipes that follow are simple, straightforward, and sensationally seasoned. Suggestions for the best time to purchase vegetables and what to look for in making your selections appear in the headnotes of many of the recipes in this chapter.

Eggplant Rolls with Tomato-Basil Sauce

[Involtini di Melanzane]

SERVES 8

Select two eggplants that are the same shape, with glossy, firm, unblemished skins. Eggplant has an affinity for oil as a sponge has for water. When sliced, liberally sprinkled with coarse salt, weighted down, and drained for 1 hour, the eggplant not only releases a dark fluid, but also decreases the amount of oil absorbed during broiling.

2 cups Tomato-Basil Sauce (page 24)	imported pecorino romano cheese
2 large purple eggplants (3 pounds)	2 tablespoons finely minced Italian flat-leaf parsley
2 tablespoons coarse salt	½ teaspoon freshly milled white pepper
4 teaspoons olive oil	
1¼ cups part-skim ricotta cheese	¼ cup fat-free egg substitute, lightly beaten
2 ounces grated part-skim mozzarella cheese (½ cup)	¼ cup minced fresh basil leaves, for garnish
3 tablespoons grated	

1. Prepare sauce at least 1 hour before salting eggplant.
2. Trim tops and bottoms of eggplants. Peel eggplant and cut length-wise into ½-inch slices, discarding the first and last slice. You will need 16 even slices, excluding the ends. Sprinkle the slices on both sides with salt and layer in colander set over a shallow bowl. Place an inverted plate on top, weight and drain for 1 hour (a 28-ounce can of tomatoes works well for weighting). Thoroughly rinse slices under cold running water. Squeeze, 2 slices at a time, to get rid of

excess moisture; thoroughly blot each slice with paper towels.

3. Adjust oven rack 4 inches from heat source and preheat on broil setting. Lightly grease broiler rack set over broiler pan with olive oil cooking spray.

4. Arrange 8 eggplant slices in a single layer in prepared pan. Brush surface of eggplant with 2 teaspoons olive oil. Broil until very lightly golden and barely tender, about 2 minutes on each side; transfer to platter. Repeat with remaining 8 slices.

5. In a medium bowl, combine ricotta, mozzarella, pecorino romano cheese, parsley, and pepper; mix well with fork. Add lightly beaten egg substitute and blend thoroughly; set filling aside.

6. Adjust oven rack to center of oven and preheat to 350°F. Line a jelly roll pan with parchment paper and lightly spray with cooking spray; set aside.

7. Place eggplant slices on work surface with narrow ends facing you. Spoon 1½ tablespoons cheese filling in center of each slice. With a metal spatula, spread filling, leaving a ½-inch margin on all sides. Working from narrow end, roll up each slice. Arrange eggplant rolls seam side down in prepared pan. Spoon 1 tablespoon Tomato-Basil sauce over each roll. Bake in preheated oven for 30 minutes. While cheese may start to ooze out a little during the first 10 minutes of baking, the rolls will be firm by the time they have finished baking.

8. Transfer rolls to platter and reheat remaining sauce. Spoon 1 tablespoon sauce over each roll, garnish with minced basil, and serve.

Per Serving: Cal. 168   Carb. 16 gm   Chol. 16 mg
              Fat 8 gm   Prot. 9 gm   Sod. 383 mg

Fennel Stew
with Carrots and Potatoes

[Spezzatino di Finocchio con Carote e Patate]

SERVES 4

Try to select fairly large, squat fennel bulbs with a pearly sheen on the outside for this stew. Serve with side dishes of Simple Green Beans (page 113) and Cauliflower Salad with Caper-Basil Vinaigrette (page 141), along with crusty Italian bread.

2 large fennel bulbs with leaves (about 2 pounds), weighed with 2 inches of leaves	3 medium all-purpose potatoes (1¼ pounds), peeled and cut into 1-inch dice
2 teaspoons olive oil	½ teaspoon crushed fennel seed
½ cup thinly sliced onions	
1 to 1¾ cups Vegetable Broth, preferably homemade (page 4), or low-sodium canned	1 tablespoon minced fresh thyme or 1 teaspoon dried thyme
4 medium peeled carrots (about ½ pound), sliced diagonally into ½-inch widths	½ teaspoon coarse salt
	½ teaspoon freshly milled black pepper

1. Remove small feathery leaves from top of fennel stalks; chop fine and reserve ¼ cup for garnish. Cut off upper stalks of bulbs and discard. Trim base of bulbs. With a vegetable peeler, lightly peel outside of bulbs to remove strings. Slice bulbs in half vertically, but do not remove center core. Cut each half into 4 wedges.

2. Blanch fennel wedges in 3 quarts of boiling water for 5 minutes. Remove with slotted spoon to colander; drain and let cool slightly. Transfer wedges to platter lined with paper towels and blot dry.

3. In a 3-quart nonstick sauté pan, heat olive oil over medium-high heat. Add fennel wedges and sauté until lightly golden, about 3 minutes on each side; transfer to platter. Add onion and sauté until lightly golden, about 5 minutes. If onion starts to stick to bottom of pan, loosen with 2 tablespoons vegetable broth.

4. Return fennel to pan and add carrots, potatoes, fennel seed, thyme, and 1 cup vegetable broth. Cook, covered, over low heat, stirring occasionally, until the vegetables are tender, about 15 to 2〔 minutes. If broth starts to evaporate in bottom of pan, stir in remaining broth, ¼ cup at a time, to keep the stew moist while cooking. Season with salt and pepper, transfer to bowl, and garnish with minced fennel leaves.

Per Serving: Cal. 171   Carb. 33 gm   Chol. 0 mg
                Fat 3 gm   Prot. 5 gm   Sod. 457 mg

Green Peppers Stuffed with Orzo

[Pepe con Ripieno di Orzo]

SERVES 4

Orzo, the rice-shaped pasta in this entrée, is sold in many supermarkets and Italian specialty stores. In some shops it is labeled melon seeds rather than orzo. Nice accompaniments to this entrée would be Grilled Portobello Mushrooms with Lemon Dressing (page 115), and Wilted Spinach with Garlic (page 122).

1¼ cups orzo
1¼ teaspoons coarse salt
1 can (16 ounces) whole
peeled tomatoes
½ cup thinly sliced scallions
3 tablespoons minced fresh
basil or 3 teaspoons dried
basil
¼ cup minced Italian flat-leaf
parsley

3 tablespoons grated
pecorino romano cheese
½ teaspoon freshly milled
black pepper
¼ cup fat-free egg substitute,
lightly beaten
4 large green bell peppers
(2 pounds), washed, dried,
halved vertically, cored,
seeded, and deribbed

1. Cook orzo in 3 quarts boiling water with 1 teaspoon coarse salt until al dente, about 9 minutes. Drain in fine mesh strainer, rinse
under cold water; set aside to cool slightly.
2. Adjust oven rack to center of oven and preheat to 350°F.
3. Drain tomatoes in strainer set over a bowl, pressing lightly on
tomatoes. Coarsely chop tomatoes and reserve 1 cup juice. In a deep
bowl, combine tomatoes, scallions, basil, parsley, cheese, remaining
¼ teaspoon salt, and pepper. Stir in lightly beaten egg substitute.
Add cooled orzo and mix well. Spoon stuffing into pepper halves and
place in a 9 × 13 × 2-inch baking pan. Spoon 1 tablespoon reserved
tomato juice over surface of each pepper. Pour remaining juice into
bottom of baking pan.
4. Cover casserole with foil and bake in preheated oven for 50 minutes. Remove foil and continue baking, basting with pan juices
every 10 minutes, until peppers are tender, about 25 minutes
longer. Remove from oven and spoon remaining pan juices over
peppers.
5. Adjust oven rack 4 inches from heat source and raise oven temperature to broil setting. Return peppers to oven and broil until a light
crust forms on surface and peppers are lightly browned around
edges. Peppers can be served either hot or at room temperature.

Per Serving: Cal. 336   Carb. 66 gm   Chol. 4 mg
               Fat 3 gm   Prot. 13 gm   Sod. 593 mg

Stuffed Summer Squash with Couscous

[Zucche Imbottite]

SERVES 4

This is a good dish to make during late summer, when large summer squash are abundant. Select squash all the same size for even cooking.

4 large yellow summer squash (about 3 pounds), scrubbed	1 tablespoon finely grated lemon zest
½ cup peeled minced carrots	½ teaspoon coarse salt
½ cup quick-cooking couscous	½ teaspoon freshly milled white pepper
⅓ cup thinly sliced scallions	¼ cup minced Italian flat-leaf parsley
½ cup coarsely chopped dark raisins	¼ cup fat-free egg substitute, lightly beaten
½ teaspoon freshly ground nutmeg	¼ cup strained fresh lemon juice

1. Cook squash in 4 quarts boiling water until barely tender, about 5 minutes. Transfer to colander, refresh under cold water, and drain thoroughly. When cool enough to handle, cut off ½ inch from stem ends of squash and trim bottoms. Slice each squash in half lengthwise. With a melon baller, scoop out seeds, leaving flesh intact; discard seeds.

2. In a heavy 2½-quart saucepan, bring 1½ cups water to a boil over high heat. Add carrots and cook until barely tender, about 3 minutes. Slowly pour in couscous and stir vigorously with wooden spoon until almost all the water is absorbed, about 30 seconds. Stir in scallions and raisins. Remove pan from heat and let couscous

mixture stand, covered, for 10 minutes. Transfer to bowl and add nutmeg, lemon zest, salt, pepper, and parsley. Cool filling to room temperature. Stir in egg substitute and mix well to combine.

3. Adjust oven rack to upper third of oven and preheat to 375°F. Lightly spray a 10½ × 15½-inch jelly roll pan with olive oil cooking spray.

4. Spoon filling into squash halves. Place squash in pan and spoon ½ tablespoon lemon juice over each stuffed squash half.

5. Bake in preheated oven until squash are tender and a light crust forms over filling, about 20 minutes. Remove from oven and let stand on cooling rack for 10 minutes. Transfer to platter and serve. Stuffed squash can be served warm or at room temperature.

Per Serving: Cal. 230   Carb. 50 gm   Chol. 0 mg
              Fat 1 gm   Prot. 9 gm   Sod. 227 mg

Tuscan Tomato and Bean Stew with Sage

[Spezzatino di Fagioli alla Toscana]

SERVES 8

Tuscany is well known for its many sage-flavored bean dishes. This is an adaptation of a recipe my grandfather Nonno Donato made frequently, especially during the fall and winter seasons. He always rubbed the toasted Italian bread with split garlic cloves before placing them in the soup plates, then spooned the bean mixture on top, and drizzled a little extra virgin oil over each portion before serving his memorable one-dish meal.

1 pound dried cannellini (white kidney beans) or Great Northern beans, picked over to remove any foreign matter, rinsed, and drained

12 large fresh sage leaves

5 large cloves garlic, unpeeled

1½ tablespoons olive oil

2 tablespoons minced garlic

1 can (28 ounces) Italian plum tomatoes, coarsely chopped, juice included

2 tablespoons minced fresh sage

½ teaspoon salt

½ teaspoon crushed red pepper flakes

8 slices Italian bread (each 1 inch thick), toasted

8 teaspoons minced Italian flat-leaf parsley for garnish

1. Place beans in a large bowl, cover with 6 cups cold water, and soak overnight. (Alternatively, you can combine beans and hot tap water in an 8-quart pot and bring to a boil over medium-high heat. Boil, uncovered, for 3 minutes. Remove from heat, cover, and let stand 1 hour.)

2. Drain beans and place in an 8-quart pot. Add 4 quarts water, the 12 sage leaves, and the 5 cloves garlic. Cover pot and bring to a boil over medium heat. Reduce heat to low and cook until beans are tender, about 1 hour. Drain beans in colander. When cool enough to handle, discard sage leaves and garlic. (Beans can be cooked 1 day ahead, placed in bowl, covered with plastic wrap, and refrigerated until needed.)

3. In a heavy 5-quart saucepan, heat olive oil over medium-low heat. Add minced garlic and sauté, stirring frequently, until lightly golden, about 2 minutes. Add tomatoes and their juice, minced sage, salt, and red pepper flakes. Turn heat to high and bring sauce to a boil, stirring frequently. Reduce heat to medium and cook, stirring frequently, until slightly thickened, about 20 minutes. Add beans to sauce, turn heat to low, and cook for an additional 10 minutes. (Stew can be prepared up to 3 hours before serving. Reheat over low heat while toasting bread.)

4. Place 1 slice of toasted bread in each soup plate, spoon bean mixture over top, garnish with parsley, and serve.

Per Serving: Cal. 285   Carb. 50 gm   Chol. 0 mg
             Fat 3 gm   Prot. 15 gm   Sod. 411 mg

Veggie Burgers with Tomato-Thyme Sauce

[Polpette Vegetarino]

SERVES 6

With the aid of a food processor, these burgers are a cinch to make. Perfect partners would be Mashed Potatoes with Garlic and Rosemary (page 120) and Brussels Sprouts with Herbed Bread Crumbs (page 105.)

1 medium leek (5 ounces), white part and 3 inches of the green, bottom trimmed, split in half lengthwise, thoroughly washed, and finely minced to make 1 cup

2 small peeled carrots (4 ounces), finely minced to make ½ cup

1 pound white mushrooms, trimmed, wiped, and finely minced

1 can (19 ounces) chick-peas, rinsed, thoroughly drained, and mashed to a paste

1 cup well-packed fresh bread crumbs from Italian or French bread, including crust, finely ground in food processor or blender

⅓ cup minced Italian flat-leaf parsley

½ teaspoon coarse salt

½ teaspoon freshly milled black pepper

½ cup fat-free egg substitute, lightly beaten

1 tablespoon olive oil

1 can (28 ounces) Italian plum tomatoes, thoroughly drained and finely chopped, juice discarded

1 tablespoon minced fresh thyme or 1 teaspoon dried thyme

1. Lightly spray a 12-inch nonstick skillet with olive oil cooking spray and heat over medium-low heat. Add ½ cup of the leeks and the car-

rots; sauté, stirring frequently, until barely tender, about 2 minutes. Add mushrooms, turn heat to medium-high, and sauté, stirring frequently, until they exude all their liquid and no moisture is left in bottom of pan, about 3 minutes. Remove from heat; stir in chickpeas, bread crumbs, parsley, salt, and pepper. Cool mixture to room temperature. Add lightly beaten egg substitute and combine well.

2. Shape into 6 round patties and place on platter lined with wax paper. Refrigerate until well chilled and firm to the touch, about 90 minutes. (Chilling will prevent burgers from falling apart while being sautéed.)

3. In a 12-inch nonstick skillet, heat 1½ teaspoons olive oil over medium-low heat. Sauté patties until golden, about 4 minutes on each side. Transfer patties to a platter. Add remaining 1½ teaspoons olive oil to skillet and stir in remaining ½ cup leeks. Sauté, stirring constantly, until barely tender, about 1 minute. Stir in tomatoes and thyme. Turn heat to high and bring sauce to a boil. As soon as it reaches a boil, turn down to medium and cook, stirring frequently, until slightly thickened, about 12 minutes. Return patties to skillet and spoon some of the sauce over each. Turn heat to low and cook, covered, until patties are heated through, about 5 minutes. Transfer to platter, spoon remaining sauce over patties, and serve.

Per Serving: Cal. 134   Carb. 19 gm   Chol. 0 mg
               Fat 4 gm   Prot. 7 gm   Sod. 374 mg

Summer Garden Stew

[Ciambotta]

SERVES 6

Here is a flavorful stew to make during the summer months when you have a bumper crop in your garden or at your local market. Italian vegetable stews (ciambotta) can vary according to the season. Bite-size pieces of cauliflower and broccoli in fall and winter or cut green beans and asparagus in spring can be substituted for the zucchini and eggplant.

1 tablespoon olive oil
½ cup peeled, thinly sliced onion
4 medium well-ripened round tomatoes (about 1 pound), blanched and peeled (see page 126 for technique) coarsely chopped, with juice included
2 tablespoons minced fresh basil
½ teaspoon coarse salt
½ teaspoon freshly milled black pepper
4 large red-skinned potatoes (about 1¼ pounds), scrubbed, ends trimmed, and cut into ½-inch dice
1 large green bell pepper (8 ounces), halved, cored, seeded, deribbed, and cut into ½-inch dice
2 medium zucchini (about 1 pound), scrubbed, ends trimmed, and cut into 1-inch dice
1 small eggplant (about 8 ounces), washed, ends trimmed, peeled, and cut into 1-inch dice
3 tablespoons minced Italian flat-leaf parsley

1. In a heavy 5-quart dutch oven, heat olive oil over medium heat. Add onion and cook, stirring frequently, until slightly softened, about 3 minutes. Stir in tomatoes, basil, salt, and pepper. Cover pan and cook sauce, stirring once or twice, for 10 minutes.

2. Add potatoes and green pepper; cover pan, turn heat to medium-low, and cook until potatoes and peppers are barely tender, about 10 minutes. Stir in zucchini and eggplant; cook, covered, stirring frequently, until all the vegetables are tender, about 10 to 15 minutes. (Stew can be made up to 3 hours before serving.) Reheat over low heat, stir in parsley, transfer to a bowl, and serve.

Per Serving: Cal. 144   Carb. 28 gm   Chol. 0 mg
                 Fat 3 gm   Prot. 4 gm   Sod. 141 mg

Winter Vegetable Stew

[Verdura in Umido]

❖

SERVES 6

Nothing is more satisfying on a cold winter night than a full-bodied stew. Excellent accompaniments would be Roasted Garlic and Fresh Herb Focaccia (page 171) along with Arugula, Mushroom, and Radish Salad (page 136).

1 large head savoy cabbage (about 2 pounds)	basil or 1 teaspoon dried basil
1 tablespoon olive oil	½ teaspoon sugar
1 medium leek (about 6 ounces), white part and 3 inches of the green, bottom trimmed, split in half lengthwise, thoroughly washed, and thinly sliced to make 1 cup	½ teaspoon coarse salt
	½ teaspoon freshly milled black pepper
	5 medium peeled carrots (9 ounces), sliced into ½-inch rounds
1 can (16 ounces) whole tomatoes, coarsely chopped, including juice	4 medium all-purpose potatoes (1½ pounds), peeled and cut into 1-inch cubes
1 tablespoon minced fresh	

1. Discard any bruised outer leaves from cabbage. Wash cabbage and blot dry. Quarter, remove core, and cut cabbage crosswise into ½-inch slices; set aside.
2. In a heavy 5½ quart saucepan, heat olive oil over low heat. Add leek and cook, stirring frequently, until soft, about 4 minutes. Stir in tomatoes and their juice, basil, sugar, salt, and pepper. Turn heat to medium-high and cook sauce, stirring frequently, for 5 minutes. Stir in cabbage, carrots, and potatoes. Continue stirring until vegetables are lightly coated with sauce. Cover pan, turn heat to low, and simmer, stirring frequently, until cabbage, carrots and potatoes

are tender, about 30 to 35 minutes. Remove from heat, transfer to bowl and serve. (This vegetable stew can be cooked up to 2 hours before serving and reheated over low heat.)

Per Serving: Cal. 164   Carb. 33 gm   Chol. 0 mg
              Fat 3 gm   Prot. 6 gm   Sod. 302 mg

Stuffed Artichokes with Sun-Dried Tomatoes and Herbs

[Carciofi Imbottiti]

SERVES 4

Artichokes are plentiful in the market from March through June. The leaves of mature artichokes should be tightly packed and bright green. Artichokes with open, spreading leaves are tough. One part of the artichoke most people discard is the stem. When trimmed, lightly peeled, and cooked, the stems have the same sweet concentrated flavoring as the heart.

4 large artichokes, each about ¾ pound (3 pounds total weight)
1 large lemon, cut in half horizontally
2 teaspoons olive oil
1 cup minced onions
1½ tablespoons minced garlic
½ cup well-packed coarsely chopped sun-dried tomatoes, not packed in oil
2 tablespoons minced fresh basil or 2 teaspoons dried basil

¼ cup minced Italian flat-leaf parsley
¼ cup grated imported pecorino romano cheese
½ teaspoon coarse salt
½ teaspoon freshly milled black pepper
1½ cups well-packed fresh bread crumbs, made from cubed Italian or French bread, including crust, coarsely ground in food processor or blender

1. Wash artichokes under cold running water, separating the leaves gently to remove any grit. Cut off stems flush with the base. Trim bottoms of stems and peel tough outer layer with a vegetable peeler. Cut stems in half lengthwise and set aside. Snap off any small or discolored leaves at the base of artichokes and cut off about 1 inch from tops. With kitchen shears, snip off about ½ inch from tip of each leaf. Rub the cut edges with lemon to prevent discoloration. Put artichokes, cut side down, in a steamer, and set steamer in a 5-quart ovenproof dutch oven containing 1 inch of water. Place stems in between artichokes. Steam, covered, over medium heat until bases are barely tender when pierced with a cake tester, about 20 minutes. Remove steamer and let artichokes cool slightly. Pour out all the cooking liquid from bottom of pan and reserve. Chop stems and set aside. With your fingers, spread the centers of artichokes to open; twist out the inner purple-tinged leaves. Remove the hairy fibers in the center of artichokes by scraping them out with a melon baller.

2. Adjust oven rack to center of oven and preheat to 375°F.

3. In a 10-inch nonstick skillet, heat olive oil over medium heat. Add onions and sauté, stirring frequently, until barely tender, about 2 minutes. Add garlic, sun-dried tomatoes, and 3 tablespoons artichoke cooking liquid. Continue cooking, stirring frequently, until onions and sun-dried tomatoes are soft, about 2 minutes. Remove from heat; stir in chopped artichoke stems, basil, parsley, 2 tablespoons of the pecorino romano cheese, salt, and pepper. Add bread crumbs and stir to combine. Stir in ¼ cup artichoke cooking liquid to moisten. In same pan, divide stuffing into 4 portions. Gently spread open leaves of artichokes. Stuff each artichoke with ¼ cup stuffing, filling centers and spaces between leaves.

4. Return artichokes to dutch oven and spoon 1 tablespoon artichoke cooking liquid over each. Bake, covered, until artichokes are extremely tender when pierced near the base with cake tester, about 20 minutes. Uncover pan, and spoon another tablespoon artichoke cooking liquid over each artichoke. Sprinkle remaining 2 tablespoons pecorino romano cheese over artichokes and continue to bake, uncovered, until tops are slightly browned and crusty, about 10 minutes. Transfer to platter and serve either hot or at room temperature.

Per Serving: Cal. 267   Carb. 49 m   Chol. 4 mg
Fat 5 gm   Prot. 12 gm   Sod. 575 mg

Asparagus with Lemon and Thyme

[Asparagi con Limone]

SERVES 6

Select asparagus all the same size so they will cook evenly. This would be a nice side dish to serve with Whole-Wheat Spaghetti with Mushrooms (page 46).

2½ pounds medium-size asparagus

½ teaspoon coarse salt

½ teaspoon freshly milled black pepper

1 tablespoon strained fresh lemon juice

2 teaspoons extra virgin olive oil

1 tablespoon minced fresh thyme or 1 teaspoon dried thyme

1 tablespoon finely grated lemon zest, for garnish

1. Cut off tough part at base of each asparagus spear on a diagonal and wash spears in cold water to remove sand. With a vegetable peeler, peel up from base of spears, leaving tips intact. Slice stalks on a diagonal so they are all the same length.

2. Put asparagus in a steamer set into a 5-quart saucepan containing 1 inch of water. Cook, covered, over medium-high heat until tender, about 4 to 5 minutes. Remove steamer and with a pair of tongs arrange asparagus on platter in an overlapping pattern. Spoon out 2 tablespoons of liquid from bottom of saucepan for making dressing.

3. In a small bowl, whisk the cooking liquid, salt, pepper, lemon juice, olive oil, and thyme. Stir with fork or whisk to combine. Spoon dressing over asparagus, garnish with grated lemon zest, and serve warm or at room temperature.

Per Serving: Cal. 49   Carb. 6 gm   Chol. 0 mg
              Fat 2 gm   Prot. 5 gm   Sod. 125 mg

Braised Broccoli di Rape with Prunes

[Broccoli di Rape Saltate con Prugne Secche]

SERVES 6

In some markets, broccoli di rape is labeled raab, rapini, or rape. Be sure to select bunches with firm stems and bright green buds. The prunes add a slightly sweet flavoring to this aggressive green.

3 large bunches broccoli di rape (about 3 pounds)
1 tablespoon extra virgin olive oil
¼ cup thinly sliced shallots
½ teaspoon coarse salt
½ teaspoon freshly milled black pepper
½ cup pitted prunes, cut into ½-inch dice

1. Remove any discolored leaves from broccoli di rape. Cut off about ½ inch of bottom stems. Wash several times in tepid water to remove grit; drain in colander. Cut off stems of broccoli di rape up to within about 1 inch of leaves. With a sharp knife, peel away the outer layer of the stem pieces. If stems are more than 4 inches in

length, slice in half crosswise. (When peeled and cooked, the stems are just as tender as the florets.)

2. In a large, heavy 6-quart saucepan, heat olive oil over medium heat. Add shallots and sauté until very lightly golden. Remove from heat and place broccoli di rape in pan. Cook, covered, over medium-high heat, stirring once or twice, until stems are barely tender, about 5 minutes. Uncover pan, turn heat to high, and continue to cook, stirring frequently, until stems are extremely tender and very little liquid is left in bottom of pan, about 2 minutes. Season with salt and pepper. Stir in prunes and cook for another 30 seconds. Transfer to platter and serve. This dish is also delicious served lukewarm.

Per Serving: Cal. 114   Carb. 20 gm   Chol. 0 mg
               Fat 3 gm   Prot. 7 gm   Sod. 244 mg

Brussels Sprouts with Herbed Bread Crumbs

[Cavoli di Bruxelles alla Mamma]

SERVES 6

The herbed bread crumbs with the brussels sprouts make an unforgettable combination for late fall.

1¼ pounds (two 10-ounce containers) brussels sprouts

1¼ teaspoons minced fresh thyme or ½ teaspoon dried thyme

1 tablespoon minced fresh basil or 1 teaspoon dried basil

1 tablespoon minced Italian flat-leaf parsley

1 tablespoon dry bread crumbs

2 teaspoons extra virgin olive oil

2 tablespoons minced shallots

½ teaspoon coarse salt

½ teaspoon freshly milled black pepper

1. Wash brussels sprouts, remove bruised outer leaves, and trim bottoms; slice each in half vertically.
2. Put brussels sprouts in a steamer set into a 5-quart saucepan containing 1 inch of water. Cook, covered, over medium-high heat until tender, about 5 to 6 minutes. Remove steamer and measure out ¼ cup liquid from bottom of saucepan; reserve liquid.
3. In a small bowl, combine thyme, basil, parsley, and bread crumbs; set aside.
4. In a 12-inch nonstick skillet, heat olive oil over low heat. Add shallots and sauté, stirring frequently, until lightly golden, about 2 minutes. Add brussels sprouts and reserved ¼ cup cooking liquid. Turn heat to medium-high and cook, stirring constantly, until no liquid is

left in pan and cut surfaces of brussels sprouts are a light golden color, about 2 minutes. Turn heat to low; season sprouts with salt and pepper. Stir in herb and bread crumb mixture and cook, stirring and tossing constantly, until brussels sprouts are coated with crumb mixture, about 20 seconds. Remove from heat, transfer to small platter, and serve.

Per Serving: Cal. 59   Carb. 9 gm   Chol. 0 mg
              Fat 2 gm   Prot. 3 gm   Sod. 154 mg

Butternut Squash with Sage

[Zucca Saporita con Salvia]

SERVES 6

Select squash with skin thick enough that it is difficult to puncture with your fingernail. Size is not a big factor in the flavor of squash; a 4-pound butternut tastes as good as one weighing 2 pounds. Steaming rather than boiling the cubed squash gives a somewhat stronger flavor (boiling tends to dilute it).

1 large butternut squash (about 3 pounds)	1 tablespoon minced fresh sage or ½ teaspoon crumbled dried sage
2 teaspoons olive oil	½ teaspoon coarse salt
1 medium leek (5 ounces), white part and 3 inches of green, trimmed, split in half lengthwise, thoroughly washed, and thinly sliced to make 1 cup	½ teaspoon freshly milled black pepper

1. Trim ends of squash and peel with vegetable peeler. Slice in half lengthwise and scoop out seeds and strings. Slice squash into 1-inch

cubes. Put squash in a steamer set into a 5-quart saucepan containing 1 inch of water. Cook, covered, over medium-high heat until tender, about 7 minutes. Remove steamer. (Squash can be cooked up to 3 hours before sautéing; transfer to bowl, cover with plastic wrap, and leave at room temperature.)

2. In a 12-inch nonstick skillet, heat olive oil over medium heat. Add leek and cook, stirring constantly, until lightly golden, about 2 minutes. Stir in cubed squash and sage. Cook, stirring constantly, until squash is heated through. Season with salt and pepper. Remove from heat, transfer to bowl, and serve.

Per Serving: Cal. 106   Carb. 24 gm   Chol. 0 mg
              Fat 2 gm   Prot. 2 gm   Sod. 132 mg

Dandelion Greens with Crispy Garlic

[Denti di Leone con Aglio]

SERVES 6

Cultivated dandelion greens resemble the wild variety found in lawns, but the dark green, saw-toothed leaves and slender stalks are much longer. Boiling the greens before sautéing dispels some of the bitterness. This flavorful green teams nicely as an accompaniment to Brown Rice with Fennel (page 74) and some crusty Italian bread.

2½ pounds dandelion greens
1   tablespoon extra virgin
    olive oil
5   large cloves garlic, peeled
    and sliced paper-thin

½   teaspoon coarse salt
½   teaspoon crushed red
    pepper flakes

1. Cut stems from base of dandelion green leaves and discard. Wash greens several times in tepid water to remove soil. After rinsing, place in an 8-quart pot. Do not add water; there will be enough clinging to the leaves. Cover pot and bring to a boil. Cook, stirring down leaves once or twice, until greens are barely tender. (Small-leaf dandelions may take 3 to 4 minutes; large-leaf dandelions may take as long as 10 to 12 minutes, depending on age and size of leaves.) Tilt the lid of the pot and pour off ⅓ cup cooking liquid; reserve liquid. Thoroughly drain dandelions in colander. When cool enough to handle, squeeze out excess moisture with your hands. Slice greens into 1½-inch lengths.

2. In a 12-inch nonstick skillet, heat olive oil over medium-high heat. Remove pan from heat, add garlic, and tilt to a 45-degree angle. With a wooden spoon, push all the garlic to one spot and sauté until lightly golden (sautéing garlic in this manner will prevent it from burning). With a slotted spoon, transfer garlic to a small plate lined with paper towel. Add greens and reserved cooking liquid to pan. Cook, covered, stirring frequently, until greens are soft to the bite, about 5 minutes. Uncover pan, turn heat to high and cook, stirring frequently, until no liquid is left in bottom of pan. Season with salt and pepper flakes; remove from heat. Stir in two-thirds of the crisp garlic. Transfer to platter, sprinkle the remaining garlic on top, and serve.

Per Serving: Cal. 104   Carb. 17 gm   Chol. 0 mg
              Fat 3 gm   Prot. 5 gm   Sod. 255 mg

Sicilian Eggplant Relish

[Caponata]

MAKES 6 CUPS

This dish exemplifies the "sweet and sour" flavoring so typical of Sicilian dishes. It can be served as a vegetable side dish or as an excellent topping for crostini on thin slices of toasted French bread, or on Polenta Canapés (page 58). One of my favorite lunches is caponata spread between halves of a crusty whole wheat roll, topped off with a little crumbled goat cheese. Caponata can be made 4 days before serving, stored in air-tight containers, and refrigerated until needed. It can also be packed into small plastic containers and frozen up to 1 month.

2 medium-size purple eggplants (about 2½ pounds), washed, ends trimmed, peeled, and cut into ½-inch cubes

2 tablespoons coarse salt

2 tablespoons olive oil

1 cup chopped red onion

1½ cups diced celery (¼-inch dice), strings removed before dicing

1 large red bell pepper (8 ounces), washed, halved, cored, deribbed, and cut into ¼-inch dice

½ cup thinly sliced medium-size California black pitted olives

5 tablespoons tomato paste

2 tablespoons red wine vinegar

1 tablespoon sugar

½ cup water

2 tablespoons minced fresh basil or 2 teaspoons dried basil

½ teaspoon freshly milled black pepper

1. Place cubed eggplant in colander set over a shallow bowl. Sprinkle with salt and toss to combine. Place an inverted plate on top of eggplant, weight, and drain for 1 hour (a 28-ounce can of tomatoes

works well for weighting). Thoroughly rinse eggplant in colander under cold running water. Take ¼ of the eggplant and squeeze with your hands to get rid of some of the moisture. Place on kitchen towel and twist towel to squeeze out all the moisture. Place in bowl and repeat with remaining eggplant.

2. Heat olive oil over medium-low heat in a 3-quart sauté pan. Add onion, celery, and bell pepper; cook, stirring frequently, until vegetables are barely tender, about 3 to 4 minutes. Stir in eggplant, turn heat to low, and continue cooking, stirring frequently, until barely tender, about 3 minutes. Remove from heat and stir in olives.

3. In a small bowl, combine tomato paste, vinegar, sugar, and water. Add to vegetable mixture and blend thoroughly.

4. Turn heat to low and cook caponata, partially covered, stirring frequently, for an additional 10 minutes. Add basil, season with pepper, and remove from heat. Let cool to room temperature before serving.

Per ¼ cup: Cal. 35   Carb. 6 gm   Chol. 0 mg

              Fat 1 gm   Prot. 1 gm   Sod. 148 mg

Braised Belgian Endive

[Brasato di Indivia del Belgio]

SERVES 4

Once you've tried this simple recipe, it is bound to become a regular in your repertoire. Nothing could be easier to cook—but you must keep an eye on the endive so that they do not overcook and become mushy.

2 teaspoons extra virgin olive oil

4 large cloves garlic, peeled and split in half

4 large unblemished heads of Belgian endive (about 1¼ pounds), wiped, bottoms trimmed, and split in half lengthwise

¾ cup dry white wine

¼ teaspoon coarse salt

¼ teaspoon freshly milled white pepper

2 tablespoons minced Italian flat-leaf parsley, for garnish

In 12-inch nonstick skillet, heat olive oil over medium heat. Add garlic and cook until lightly golden, about 1 minute. Remove pan from heat and place endive in pan, cut sides down. Arrange cut garlic between slices. Add wine, cover pan, and cook over medium heat until endive are barely tender when pierced at base with a cake tester, about 8 to 10 minutes. Uncover pan and discard garlic with a slotted spoon. Raise heat to high and cook until cut surfaces of endive are lightly golden and no liquid is left in bottom of pan, about 2 to 3 minutes. Transfer to platter with cut sides up. Season with salt and pepper. Garnish with parsley and serve either hot or at room temperature.

Per Serving: Cal. 45   Carb. 5 gm   Chol. 0 mg
Fat 2 gm   Prot. 1 gm   Sod. 102 mg

Escarole and Kidney Beans

[Scarola alla Amadea]

SERVES 6

My daughter Amy loves escarole and has developed this recipe to serve over cooked brown rice. It is equally as good served over steaming hot bowls of Basic Polenta (page 54). You can substitute curly endive for the escarole. This dish can be prepared up to 3 hours before serving. Reheat, covered, over low heat.

2 large heads escarole (about 2½ pounds)	1 can (16 ounces) dark red kidney beans, rinsed and well drained
1 tablespoon extra virgin olive oil	½ teaspoon coarse salt
½ cup thinly sliced onion	½ teaspoon freshly milled black pepper
½ cup diced peeled carrots	
1 tablespoon minced garlic	

1. Discard any wilted or bruised leaves from escarole. Separate leaves and trim off about 2 inches of tough bottom ends of greens. Slice greens into 3-inch lengths and wash several times in tepid water to get rid of grit. Place escarole in a 6-quart pot. Do not add water; the final rinse water clinging to leaves will be sufficient to steam them. Cook, covered, over high heat, pushing leaves down with wooden spoon once or twice, until stems are tender, about 5 minutes. Thoroughly drain in colander.

2. In a 12-inch nonstick skillet, heat olive oil over low heat. Sauté onion and carrots until slightly softened, about 3 minutes. Add garlic and sauté for another minute. Add escarole and cook, covered, over medium heat, stirring frequently, until extremely soft, about 6 minutes. Stir in kidney beans and season with salt and pepper; cook an additional 5 minutes, partially covered.

Per Serving: Cal. 107   Carb. 16 gm   Chol. 0 mg
               Fat 3 gm   Prot. 6 gm   Sod. 249 mg

Simple Green Beans

[Fagiolini Verdi alla Toscana]

SERVES 6

Try this quick and delicious vegetable preparation with 4 cups broccoli florets cut into 1-inch pieces, or 4 medium trimmed zucchini sliced into 1-inch rounds, in place of the green beans.

1¾ pounds green beans, washed and trimmed	½ teaspoon coarse salt
1 large clove garlic, peeled and split in half	½ teaspoon freshly milled black pepper
1 tablespoon extra virgin olive oil	

1. Put green beans in a steamer set into a 5-quart saucepan containing 1 inch of water. Cook, covered, over medium-high heat until tender, about 5 to 6 minutes. Remove steamer. Spoon out 2 tablespoons of liquid from bottom of saucepan and reserve.
2. While green beans are cooking, rub bottom and sides of a deep bowl with split garlic; discard garlic.
3. Transfer cooked beans to prepared bowl. Toss beans with 2 tablespoons of reserved cooking liquid and the olive oil. Season with salt and pepper and serve.

Per Serving: Cal. 57   Carb. 9 gm   Chol. 0 mg
               Fat 2 gm   Prot. 2 gm   Sod. 129 mg

Kale with Raisins and Pine Nuts

[Verza alla Lovi]

✦

SERVES 6

Select deep green bunches of kale with slightly moist leaves; avoid overly dry, browned, yellowed leaves. Kale is available all year, but is most flavorful during the late fall and winter seasons. This hearty vegetable is an excellent accompaniment to Polenta Pie with Mushroom Filling (page 63).

1¾	pounds kale	½	teaspoon freshly milled
1	tablespoon olive oil		black pepper
½	cup thinly sliced red onion	2	tablespoons pine nuts,
¼	cup dark raisins		lightly toasted
½	teaspoon coarse salt		

1. Kale leaves should always be stripped from their stems and tough center ribs. Hold the stem with one hand and pull the leaves off with the other hand to remove stems and ribs. Wash several times in tepid water. Remove from final rinse water and place in an 8-quart pot. Do not add water; there will be enough clinging to the leaves. Cover pot and bring to a boil. Cook, stirring down leaves once or twice, until kale is tender. (Small-leaf kale may take about 4 to 5 minutes; large-leaf kale will take a little longer.) Tilt the lid of the pot and pour off ⅓ cup cooking liquid; reserve liquid. Thoroughly drain kale in colander. When cool enough to handle, cut kale into 1-inch strips and set aside.

2. In a 12-inch nonstick skillet, heat olive oil over low heat. Add onion and sauté, stirring frequently, until lightly golden, about 3 minutes. Add kale and its reserved cooking liquid. Turn heat up to medium-high and cook, stirring constantly, until no liquid is left in bottom of

pan, about 1 minute. Stir in raisins and cook until plumped, about 20 seconds. Season with salt and pepper; remove from heat. Stir in toasted pine nuts, transfer to bowl, and serve.

Per Serving: Cal. 100   Carb. 15 gm   Chol. 0 mg
Fat 4 gm   Prot. 4 gm   Sod. 159 mg

Grilled Portobello Mushrooms with Lemon Dressing

[Funghi alla Griglia]

SERVES 6

This is one of my favorite ways to serve portobello mushrooms. They can be served hot off the grill or at room temperature. Any leftovers make great candidates for a sandwich, especially on crusty Italian bread.

4 large portobello mushrooms (about 2 pounds)	½ teaspoon freshly milled black pepper
1 tablespoon extra virgin olive oil	3 tablespoons snipped chives or tender top green part of scallions
3 tablespoons strained fresh lemon juice	2 tablespoons minced Italian flat-leaf parsley
½ teaspoon coarse salt	

1. Slice stems off at base of mushrooms and discard. Wipe mushrooms with a damp cloth to remove any grit.

2. Lightly grease charcoal or gas grill rack with olive oil cooking spray. Preheat charcoal grill until coals have turned a gray ashy color, or preheat gas grill according to manufacturer's suggested time on medium-high heat. (Mushrooms can also be broiled 4 inches from heat source in oven.)

3. Lightly brush mushrooms caps with 1½ teaspoons of the olive oil. Place on grill with cap sides down. Grill until caps are tender, about 3 minutes, rotating clockwise with wide metal spatula once or twice to prevent burned spots. Brush under surfaces (gills) with remaining 1½ teaspoons oil and flip each mushroom over. Continue to grill until undersides are tender, about 2 minutes. Transfer to cutting board and slice into ½-inch strips. Arrange on platter in a slightly overlapping pattern and drizzle with lemon juice. Season with salt and pepper, sprinkle with chives and parsley, and serve.

Per Serving:	Cal. 56	Carb. 7 gm	Chol. 0 mg
	Fat 3 gm	Prot. 3 gm	Sod. 128 mg

Sautéed Mushrooms with Sun-Dried Tomatoes

[Funghi Saltati con Pomodoro Secco]

SERVES 4

Select white mushrooms with smooth, unblemished skins. The caps should be closed with no gills showing around stems.

2	teaspoons extra virgin olive oil		not packed in oil, sliced diagonally into ¼-inch strips
2	teaspoons minced garlic	½	cup dry vermouth
1	pound medium-size white mushrooms, stemmed, wiped, and sliced ¼ inch thick	¼	teaspoon coarse salt
		¼	teaspoon freshly milled black pepper
¼	cup sun-dried tomatoes,	2	tablespoons minced Italian flat-leaf parsley

In a 12-inch nonstick skillet, heat olive oil over low heat. Add garlic and sauté until lightly golden. Add mushrooms, sun-dried tomatoes, and dry vermouth. Turn heat to medium-high and cook, stirring frequently, until mushrooms are tender and no liquid is left in bottom of pan, about 2 to 3 minutes. Season with salt and pepper; remove from heat. Stir in parsley, transfer to small platter, and serve.

Per Serving: Cal. 87 Carb. 10 gm Chol. 0 mg
Fat 3 gm Prot. 3 gm Sod. 104 mg

Stuffed Baked Potatoes with Sun-Dried Tomatoes and Dill

[Patate alla Anna]

❖

SERVES 4

Serve these creamy twice-baked potatoes with Wilted Spinach with Garlic (page 122) and Broccoli Salad with Lemon-Honey Dressing (page 140).

4 large russet baking potatoes (about 2¾ pounds)	3 tablespoons skim milk
¼ cup sun-dried tomatoes, not packed in oil	½ cup part-skim ricotta cheese
2 tablespoons minced scallions	¼ cup fat-free egg substitute, lightly beaten
1 tablespoon minced fresh dill or 1 teaspoon dried dill	¼ teaspoon coarse salt
	¼ teaspoon freshly milled black pepper

1. Adjust oven rack to center of oven and preheat to 400°F.
2. Scrub potatoes with a brush under running water and blot dry. Pierce potatoes several times with fork and place on a small baking sheet. Bake until skins are crisp and potatoes are cooked through when pierced with a cake tester, about 1 hour. Leave oven on.
3. While potatoes are baking, place sun-dried tomatoes in a bowl and pour on boiling water to cover. Let stand 2 minutes to soften; thoroughly drain and blot dry. When cool enough to handle, dice fine. Transfer to small bowl, and combine with scallions and dill; set aside.
4. Transfer baked potatoes to cutting board and cool slightly. Cut off laterally top third of potatoes. With a melon baller, carefully scoop out potato pulp, leaving ¼-inch-thick shells. Scoop out pulp from tops of potatoes; discard tops. Place potato pulp in bowl of electric

mixer fitted with whip attachment. Add milk and ricotta. Run machine on medium speed until potato mixture is smooth and creamy. Stop machine once and scrape inside of bowl with rubber spatula. Add lightly beaten egg substitute, salt, and pepper; beat on medium speed until blended. Stir in sun-dried tomato mixture. Spoon potato mixture back into shells, mounding in center. Smooth top surfaces with narrow metal spatula. (Potatoes can be assembled up to 3 hours before returning to oven for final baking.)
5. Place potatoes on small baking sheet and return to 400°F. preheated oven; bake until top surfaces are golden brown, about 25 to 30 minutes. Transfer to small platter and serve.

Per Serving: Cal. 324   Carb. 63 gm   Chol. 9 mg
                Fat 3 gm   Prot. 12 gm   Sod. 191 mg

Mashed Potatoes with Garlic and Rosemary

[Involtini di Patate]

❖

SERVES 6

Here is a flavorful winter dish to make for anyone who loves garlic, a perfect partner with Braised Broccoli di Rape with Prunes (page 103) and Sautéed Mushrooms with Sun-dried Tomatoes (page 117).

4 large russet baking potatoes (about 2¾ pounds), peeled and cut into 1-inch cubes
5 large garlic cloves, peeled and sliced in half
1 cup Vegetable Broth, preferably homemade (page 4), or low-sodium canned, heated
½ teaspoon coarse salt

½ teaspoon freshly milled white pepper
1 tablespoon minced fresh rosemary or 1 teaspoon chopped dried rosemary
¼ cup well-packed freshly grated imported Parmesan cheese
2 tablespoons minced Italian flat-leaf parsley, for garnish

1. Place potatoes and garlic in a 5-quart pot and add enough cold water to cover by 1 inch. Bring to a boil, cover, and cook until potatoes are very tender, about 25 to 30 minutes. Thoroughly drain in colander.

2. Put potatoes, garlic, and ½ cup of the heated vegetable stock in bowl of electric mixer fitted with whip attachment. Beat on low speed until potatoes begin to break up. Stop machine and scrape down inside of bowl with rubber spatula. Add remaining heated broth and beat on medium speed until potato mixture is smooth and creamy. Add salt, pepper, rosemary, and Parmesan cheese; beat on medium speed until well blended. Transfer to bowl, garnish with parsley, and serve.

Per Serving: Cal. 172   Carb. 36 gm   Chol. 2 mg
              Fat 1 gm   Prot. 5 gm   Sod. 261 mg

Braised Romaine Lettuce

[Brasato di Lattuga]

SERVES 6

You may substitute any type of leaf lettuce, escarole, or curly endive for the romaine in this braised mixture. It is also excellent spooned over bowls of hot steaming polenta or cooked brown rice, topped off with a little grated pecorino romano cheese, as an entrée.

3	large heads romaine lettuce (about 4 pounds)		strings removed before slicing
1	tablespoon olive oil	1	tablespoon minced garlic
½	cup thinly sliced yellow onion	½	teaspoon coarse salt
½	cup thinly sliced celery,	½	teaspoon freshly milled black pepper

1. Separate romaine leaves and cut off about 1 inch from bottom of greens. Trim off any bruised tips of leaves. Wash several times in tepid water to remove grit. Drain well and blot or spin dry. Cut leaves crosswise into 1-inch lengths; set aside. (If leaves are exceptionally large, slice down the middle before cutting crosswise.)

2. In a heavy 5-quart saucepan, heat olive oil over medium heat. Add onion and celery; sauté, stirring frequently, until tender-crisp, about 2 minutes. Add garlic and sauté for an additional 30 seconds. Stir in romaine and cook, covered, pushing greens down with wooden spoon once or twice, until they are tender, about 10 to 12 minutes. Uncover pan, turn heat to high, and cook, stirring fre-

quently, until no liquid is left in bottom of pan. Season with salt and pepper. Remove from heat, transfer to bowl, and serve.

Per Serving: Cal. 75   Carb. 9 gm   Chol. 0 mg
              Fat 3 gm   Prot. 5 gm   Sod. 154 mg

Wilted Spinach with Garlic

[Spinaci con Aglio]

SERVES 6

This is a very simple way to prepare spinach. Wilting the spinach with boiling water preserves the vivid color of the greens and also keeps them tender-crisp. (This is also an excellent way to cook stemmed watercress.)

2 pounds fresh spinach with stems, or 2 bags (10 ounces each) fresh spinach leaves	2 teaspoons minced garlic
	½ teaspoon coarse salt
	½ teaspoon freshly milled black pepper
2 teaspoons extra virgin olive oil	

1. Discard stems from spinach. Wash leaves several times in tepid water to remove grit. Remove half of the spinach from final rinse water and place in a deep colander. Place colander in sink.
2. While you are washing spinach, bring 7 cups of water to a boil. (An 8-cup tea kettle is recommended.) Pour half of the boiling water over spinach in colander until it is wilted, about 20 seconds. Thoroughly drain; transfer wilted spinach to a deep bowl. Repeat with remaining spinach and transfer to bowl with first batch. With a wooden spoon, press spinach down in bowl and pour off any accumulated liquid from bottom of bowl.

3. In a 12-inch nonstick skillet, heat olive oil over medium heat. Add garlic and sauté, stirring constantly, until lightly golden, about 30 seconds. Stir in spinach, turn heat to high, and cook, stirring constantly, until heated through, about 30 seconds. Season with salt and pepper. Remove from heat, transfer to bowl, and serve. (Spinach can be served hot or at room temperature.)

Per Serving: Cal. 40   Carb. 4 gm   Chol. 0 mg
            Fat 2 gm   Prot. 3 gm   Sod. 208 mg

Swiss Chard with Balsamic Vinegar

[Bietole con Aceto Balsamico]

SERVES 4

This is a very simple way to prepare either green or ruby Swiss chard. Select crisp-stalked bunches with firm, bright leaves.

2 pounds Swiss chard	¼ teaspoon freshly milled black pepper
2 teaspoons extra virgin olive oil	
½ cup thinly sliced onion	2 tablespoons balsamic vinegar
¼ teaspoon coarse salt	

1. Trim off any wilted or discolored edges from chard leaves; cut leaves from stems. Trim bottoms of stems. Wash leaves and stems separately in tepid water several times to remove grit; drain well. Slice stems diagonally into ½-inch widths. (If stems are wider than 1 inch, lightly peel with a vegetable peeler to remove fibrous strings

and halve lengthwise before slicing.) Slice leaves crosswise into 1-inch lengths.

2. In a heavy 5-quart saucepan, heat olive oil over low heat. Add onion and chard stems. Cover and cook, stirring frequently, until stems are tender, about 15 to 20 minutes. Add chard leaves and stir to combine. Cover and cook over medium heat, stirring frequently until tender, about 5 to 10 minutes. Season with salt and pepper. Stir in vinegar and remove from heat. Cover pan and let stand for 5 minutes before serving.

Per Serving: Cal. 69   Carb. 10 gm   Chol. 0 mg
              Fat 3 gm   Prot. 4 gm   Sod. 536 mg

Technique for Roasting Peppers

W) hen large, thick-skinned bell peppers are bountiful, buy several pounds. Roast the peppers, peel, and leave in large strips. Place in plastic containers and freeze until needed. They can be kept frozen up to 4 months. Defrost peppers 4 hours or overnight in refrigerator before using.

Select large red, yellow, orange, or green bell peppers for roasting, each weighing at least 6 to 8 ounces. Look for peppers that are firm and bright, unbruised, and unwrinkled.

1. Adjust oven rack to 4 inches from broiler and preheat to broil setting.
2. Wash peppers in cold water; blot dry with paper towels. Slice off both ends of each pepper to make a cylinder. (Discard top and bottom ends or save for another use.) Cut each pepper in half lengthwise. Remove seeds, and carefully slice off any protruding ribs. Slice each halved pepper into three even lengthwise strips.
3. Place pepper strips, cut sides down, on broiler rack set over broiler pan. Broil peppers until partially charred, about 5 minutes. Remove from oven, wrap in paper towels, and place in a plastic bag. Secure the end with a twist tie and let stand for at least 1 hour to cool. Remove from bag and peel peppers with a small paring knife. Pat dry with paper towels and cut into desired lengths.

Technique for Blanching Tomatoes

Select bright red plum or round tomatoes that are well ripened with unblemished skins for blanching. If tomatoes are slightly underripe when you buy them, place them in a basket and leave at room temperature for a few days to ripen. When in season you may want to purchase several pounds. (After blanching, coring, and seeding tomatoes, they can be packed in pint-size plastic containers, along with juice, and kept frozen up to 6 months.)

Cut a cross in the bottom end of each tomato (this will make peeling easier after blanching). Blanch about 4 tomatoes at a time in 3 quarts rapidly boiling water, until the skins start to separate from the flesh, about 30 to 40 seconds. With a slotted spoon, transfer tomatoes to colander and cool to room temperature. If recipe calls for more tomatoes, return water to a boil and repeat with remaining tomatoes. With a small paring knife, peel skins and cut out center core; discard skins and core. After all the tomatoes are peeled, slice each in half *crosswise* (not through the core). Lightly squeeze each half in a strainer set over a bowl to release most of the seeds and juice. Poke out any remaining seeds with your finger; discard seeds and reserve juice. Tomatoes are now ready to be cut, chopped, or diced and combined with reserved juices, if recipe specifies *with juices included.*

Sicilian-Style Baked Turnips

[Strati di Rape alla Siciliana]

SERVES 6

This layered turnip dish, laced with onion, tomato, and oregano, is an excellent partner to Polenta with Leeks and Sage (page 62).

4 medium stemmed turnips (about 1¾ pounds), washed, peeled, and sliced into ⅛-inch thin rounds

1 medium red onion (about 5 ounces), peeled and sliced into paper-thin rounds

7 large, well-ripened plum tomatoes (about 1¼ pounds), washed, ends trimmed, and sliced into ¼-inch rounds

2 teaspoons extra virgin olive oil

½ teaspoon coarse salt

½ teaspoon freshly milled black pepper

1 tablespoon minced fresh oregano or 1 teaspoon dried oregano

1. Adjust oven rack to center of oven and preheat to 350°F. Lightly grease a 9 × 13 × 2-inch ovenproof baking dish with olive oil cooking spray.
2. Arrange half of the turnips in an overlapping pattern in prepared baking dish. Scatter half of the onion slices over top. Arrange half of the plum tomatoes in a single layer over onions. Brush surface of tomatoes with half of the olive oil. Sprinkle half of the salt, pepper, and oregano over top. Arrange second layer the same as first with remaining ingredients. Cover with foil and bake in preheated oven until turnips are tender when tested with the tip of a knife, about 55 to 60 minutes. Remove from oven and discard foil.
3. Adjust oven rack to 4 inches from heat source and preheat to broil setting.
4. Return turnips to oven and broil until a light crust forms on surface

of tomatoes, about 3 to 4 minutes. This turnip dish can be served hot or at room temperature.

Per Serving: Cal. 72   Carb. 13 gm   Chol. 0 mg
                 Fat 2 gm   Prot. 2 gm   Sod. 205 mg

Grilled White Eggplant

[Melanzane Arostiti]

SERVES 4

This is a good dish to make during the summer months when white eggplant is plentiful. The flesh and skin of the white eggplant tend to be firmer than the purple globe variety, which makes them an excellent choice for grilling. They can also be broiled 4 inches from heat source in the oven.

2   medium round white eggplants (about 2½ pounds)

2   teaspoons extra virgin olive oil

1   tablespoon balsamic vinegar

½   teaspoon coarse salt

½   teaspoon freshly milled black pepper

3   tablespoons snipped fresh chives or tender green tops of scallions

2   tablespoons minced fresh thyme or 2 teaspoons dried thyme

1. Wash and dry eggplant; trim both ends. Slice each eggplant into four ¾-inch-thick rounds. Place slices between layers of paper towel and press lightly to release some of the moisture.
2. Lightly grease charcoal or gas grill rack with vegetable cooking spray. Preheat charcoal grill until coals have turned a gray ashy color or preheat gas grill according to manufacturer's suggested time on medium-high heat.

3. Lightly brush eggplant slices with 1 teaspoon olive oil. Place on grill with oiled side down. Grill eggplant until undersides are lightly golden, about 2 to 3 minutes; rotating clockwise with wide metal spatula once or twice to prevent burned spots. Brush tops of eggplant slices with remaining 1 teaspoon olive oil and flip each slice over. Continue to grill until underside is lightly golden, about 2 minutes, rotating once again with metal spatula. Transfer to platter and arrange in single layer. Lightly brush with balsamic vinegar. Season with salt and pepper, sprinkle with chives and thyme, and serve. This dish is also excellent served at room temperature.

Per Serving: Cal. 90   Carb. 17 gm   Chol. 0 mg
                   Fat 3 gm   Prot. 3 gm   Sod. 194 mg

Yellow Wax Beans with Olives and Sage

[Fagiolini Arlena]

SERVES 6

This recipe was created by my very dear friend and colleague, Arlene Coria Ward. The olives and sage add zesty flavor to the wax beans.

1¾ pounds yellow wax beans, washed and trimmed

1 tablespoon extra virgin olive oil

¼ cup minced red onion

8 large calamata olives, pitted and coarsely chopped to make 2 tablespoons

1 tablespoon minced fresh sage or 1 teaspoon crumbled dried sage

½ teaspoon coarse salt

½ teaspoon freshly milled black pepper

4 short sprigs fresh sage, for garnish

1. Put wax beans in a steamer set into a 5-quart saucepan containing 1 inch of water. Cook, covered, over medium-high heat until barely tender, about 3 minutes. Remove steamer and let beans cool to room temperature. Cut beans diagonally into 2-inch lengths. Measure out and reserve 3 tablespoons liquid from bottom of saucepan.

2. In 12-inch nonstick skillet, heat olive oil over medium heat. Add onion and sauté until lightly golden, about 3 minutes. Add wax beans and reserved liquid. Cook, stirring frequently, until tender and no liquid is left in bottom of pan, about 2 to 3 minutes. Stir in olives and minced sage; cook for an additional 30 seconds. Season with salt and pepper; remove from heat. Transfer to platter and garnish with sprigs of fresh sage.

Per Serving: Cal. 80   Carb. 9 gm   Chol. 0 mg
                Fat 5 gm   Prot. 2 gm   Sod. 325 mg

Salads

Salad in an Italian household is never served before the first course unless it is a composed salad that stands on its own as an entrée, such as Tricolor Pasta Salad, Rice and Double Bean Salad, or Lentil Salad with Orange Mint Dressing. If you are serving pasta, polenta, or risotto as an entrée, the salad is usually served as the second course. If you serve a vegetable entrée, the salad may be served along with this dish.

Whether I offer salad with a meal or after a meal, I insist on serving it in individual bowls or on a separate plate so that the delicate dressing will not mingle with the entrée.

Whether you are making a complex salad of roasted or steamed vegetables or a simple lettuce and tomato salad, always bear in mind the contrasting flavors and textures. The peppery spice of watercress and the bitter bite of arugula, radicchio, or dandelion greens make wonderful additions to the more subtle Boston, romaine, green, or red leaf curly lettuces. Be selective and attentive as you vary textures, tastes, and colors. Three or four different lettuces make a great balance. Once the salad is dressed, you'll have a great marriage of flavorings.

This brings us to the traditional dressing, one part vinegar to three parts olive oil. Since a few tablespoons of salad dressing can turn a light meal into one's daily allowance of fat, I have altered these recipes by replacing some of the extra virgin olive oil with the flavor-infused juices in which the vegetables had been either steamed or roasted—adding a variety of vinegars, or a citric selection of lemon, orange, or tomato juice, incorporating a slight showering of fresh herbs, minced onion, chives, or garlic to enhance the harmonious blending of the dressings.

Just remember, the contents of a salad bowl need not be predictable; they can offer variety and an element of surprise. These recipes are simple blueprints for tossing a perfect salad, so feel free to add and subtract ingredients according to season, availability, appetite, and whim.

In addition to the typical salad of garden-fresh greens, a number of salad recipes incorporating vegetables, beans, and fruits follow. More substantial salads that serve as main courses appear in the chapters on pasta and rice.

Artichoke Heart, Lima Bean, and Fennel Salad

[Insalata di Carciofi, Fagiolini, e Finocchio]

❖

SERVES 6

A good late fall and winter salad to make when fresh fennel is always available.

1 package (9 ounces) frozen artichoke hearts, defrosted and well drained

1 package (10 ounces) frozen baby lima beans, defrosted and well drained

1 medium fennel bulb with leaves (about 12 ounces) weighed with 2 inches of stalk

½ cup thinly sliced scallions,

white part and 3 inches of the green

2 tablespoons white wine vinegar

½ teaspoon sugar

½ teaspoon coarse salt

½ teaspoon freshly milled white pepper

1 tablespoon extra virgin olive oil

1. Put artichoke hearts and lima beans in a steamer set into a 5-quart saucepan containing 1 inch of water. Cook, covered, over medium-high heat until both are tender, about 6 minutes. Remove steamer and let artichokes and lima beans cool to room temperature. Measure out 3 tablespoons of liquid from bottom of saucepan and reserve for dressing.

2. Remove small feathery leaves from top of fennel stalks, finely chop, and reserve ¼ cup for garnish. Cut off and discard stalks. Trim base of bulb. With a vegetable peeler, lightly peel outside of bulb to remove strings. Slice bulb in half vertically and remove center core with a V cut. Thinly slice bulb lengthwise into 1-inch strips. Trans-

fer to a salad bowl. Add artichoke hearts, lima beans, and scallions; lightly toss to combine.

3. In a small bowl, combine reserved cooking liquid, vinegar, sugar, salt, and pepper. Stir with fork or whisk. Add olive oil and whisk until dressing is well blended. Drizzle dressing over salad and toss gently. Cover with plastic wrap and refrigerate until chilled, about 1 hour. (Salad can be prepared up to 3 hours before serving.) Toss once again, garnish with fennel leaves, and serve.

Per Serving: Cal. 110   Carb. 18 gm   Chol. 0 mg
              Fat 3 gm   Prot. 5 gm   Sod. 206 mg

Green Bean and Chick-Pea Salad

[Insalata di Fagiolini e Ceci]

SERVES 6

If you prefer, you may substitute dark red kidney beans for the chick-peas. This salad is a good accompaniment to Zucchini-Rice Soup (page 17) with some crusty Italian bread.

1½ pounds green beans, washed and trimmed

1 can (16 ounces) chick-peas, rinsed and drained

½ cup paper-thin slices red onion

2 teaspoons balsamic vinegar

½ teaspoon coarse salt

½ teaspoon freshly milled black pepper

1 tablespoon extra virgin olive oil

1 tablespoon minced fresh thyme or 1 teaspoon dried thyme

1. Put green beans in a steamer set into a 5-quart saucepan containing 1 inch of water. Cook, covered, over medium-high heat until tender, about 5 to 7 minutes. Remove steamer and let beans cool to room temperature. Cut beans diagonally into 2-inch lengths and place in bowl. Spoon out 2 tablespoons of liquid from bottom of saucepan and reserve for dressing.

2. To remove skins from chick-peas, squeeze each one gently between thumb and forefinger to slip off the skins; discard skins. Transfer to bowl with green beans; add onion and toss gently to combine.

3. In a small bowl, combine reserved cooking liquid, vinegar, salt, and pepper. Stir with fork or small whisk. Add olive oil and thyme; whisk until dressing is well blended. Drizzle dressing over salad, toss gently and serve. (Salad can be prepared up to 2 hours before serving. Cover with plastic wrap and let stand at room temperature. Gently toss again before serving.)

Per Serving: Cal. 109   Carb. 16 gm   Chol. 0 mg
                    Fat 4 gm   Prot. 5 gm   Sod. 213 mg

Arugula, Mushroom, and Radish Salad

[Insalata alla Giovanna]

❖

SERVES 6

Make this salad when you can find white button mushrooms with tight-fitting stems. Blanching the mushrooms in a vinegar-water solution helps retain their pure white color. This is my daughter Joanne's favorite salad, which she serves quite often during the winter months.

2½ cups water

3 tablespoons distilled white vinegar

8 ounces white button mushrooms, wiped and stemmed

1 large bunch arugula, stems discarded, thoroughly washed, spun dry, and cut into bite-size pieces to make about 5 cups, loosely packed

1 cup shredded radishes, washed and trimmed before shredding (can be

shredded in food processor fitted with shredding disk)

3 tablespoons snipped chives or tender tops of scallions

½ teaspoon sugar

¼ teaspoon coarse salt

½ teaspoon freshly milled black pepper

1½ tablespoons strained fresh lemon juice

1½ tablespoons extra virgin olive oil

3 tablespoons coarsely grated mellow Asiago cheese

1. In a 2½-quart saucepan, bring water and distilled vinegar to a boil. Drop mushroom caps into boiling vinegar-water mixture. When water returns to a boil, blanch mushrooms for 30 seconds. Drain in strainer and cool to room temperature. Place mushrooms in center of towel and squeeze out all the excess moisture. Thinly slice mush-

room caps, place in salad bowl, and combine with arugula and radishes.

2. Put chives, sugar, salt, pepper, and lemon juice in a small bowl; stir with a fork or small whisk to combine. Add olive oil and whisk until dressing is well blended. Drizzle the dressing over salad and toss gently. Sprinkle Asiago cheese over top and serve.

Per Serving: Cal. 60   Carb. 4 gm   Chol. 2 mg
                 Fat 4 gm   Prot. 2 gm   Sod. 108 mg

Four Bean Salad

[Insalata di Fagioli]

SERVES 10

This is a streamlined version of a salad I first tasted at a picnic at the home of my friend Emi Lou Havas. Select the best quality premium canned beans you can find, so that when the salad is tossed the beans will remain firm.

1	can (16-ounces) small black beans	6	medium well-ripened plum tomatoes (about 12 ounces)
1	can (16 ounces) dark red kidney beans	2	tablespoons balsamic vinegar
1	can (16 ounces) small lima beans	1	teaspoon Dijon-style mustard
1	can (16 ounces) small white beans	1	teaspoon sugar
½	cup thinly sliced scallions	½	teaspoon coarse salt
1	tablespoon minced fresh thyme or 1 teaspoon dried thyme	½	teaspoon freshly milled black pepper
½	cup minced Italian flat-leaf parsley	1½	tablespoons extra virgin olive oil

1. Place all the canned beans in a large colander and rinse under cold running water. Thoroughly drain beans and blot dry. Gently stir in scallions, thyme, and parsley.
2. Wash tomatoes and blot dry. Slice each in half horizontally and core. Lightly squeeze each half in a strainer set over a bowl to release most of the seeds and juice. Poke out any remaining seeds with your finger; discard seeds, and reserve ⅓ cup juice for dressing. Slice tomatoes into ½-inch dice and add to bean mixture.
3. Put the reserved tomato juice, the vinegar, mustard, sugar, salt, and pepper in a small bowl. Stir with fork or whisk. Slowly add olive oil and whisk until blended. Gently toss dressing with salad, cover with plastic wrap, and refrigerate until well chilled, about 1 hour. (Salad can be made up to 3 hours ahead). Gently toss once again before serving.

Per Serving: Cal. 111   Carb. 17 gm   Chol. 0 mg
               Fat 2 gm   Prot. 6 gm   Sod. 271 mg

Roasted Beet Salad

[Insalata di Barbabietola Arrostita]

SERVES 6

Roasting the beets wrapped in foil not only ensures that no flavor is lost but also preserves the vivid ruby color.

1½ pounds (about 12) medium-size beets, weighed with 1 inch of stems
3 tablespoons snipped fresh chives or tender green tops of scallions
2 tablespoons minced fresh mint leaves

1 tablespoon balsamic vinegar
½ teaspoon coarse salt
½ teaspoon freshly milled black pepper
1 tablespoon extra virgin olive oil

1. Adjust oven rack to center of oven and preheat to 375°F.
2. Trim beets, leaving 1 inch of the stems attached. Scrub beets with vegetable brush under running water. Wrap each beet in aluminum foil and place in a 9 × 13 × 2-inch baking pan. Add ½-inch of hot water to bottom of pan. Roast until beets are tender when pierced through foil with a metal cake tester, about 50 to 70 minutes. Unwrap the beets carefully and pour any beet juices accumulated in the foil into a small bowl. Reserve 2 tablespoons of beet juice for dressing. While beets are still warm, but cool enough to handle, slice off stems and slip off the skins. Halve beets and slice into ½-inch wedges. Transfer to bowl; combine with chives and mint.
3. In small bowl, combine the reserved beet juice with vinegar, salt, and pepper; stir with fork or small whisk to combine. Add olive oil and whisk until dressing is well blended. Toss dressing with beets and

serve. Salad can be made up to 3 hours before serving. Cover with plastic wrap and refrigerate. Toss once again before serving.

Per Serving: Cal. 55   Carb. 8 gm   Chol. 0 mg
              Fat 2 gm   Prot. 1 gm   Sod. 177 mg

Broccoli Salad with Lemon-Honey Dressing

[Insalata di Broccoli]

SERVES 4

To prevent bleached spots from the vinaigrette on the florets, the dressing should be spooned over the salad just before serving.

6 cups bite-size pieces broccoli florets with ¼ inch of stems included, washed and drained

1 tablespoon strained fresh lemon juice

1½ teaspoons honey

1 teaspoon finely grated peeled fresh ginger

2 tablespoons finely minced shallots

¼ teaspoon coarse salt

¼ teaspoon freshly milled black pepper

2 teaspoons extra virgin olive oil

2 tablespoons finely grated lemon zest, for garnish

1. Put broccoli florets in a steamer set into a 5-quart saucepan containing 1 inch of water. Cook, covered, over medium-high heat, until florets are barely tender, about 5 minutes. Remove steamer and let florets cool to room temperature. Spoon out 1½ tablespoons of liquid from bottom of saucepan and reserve for dressing. Arrange

broccoli on a platter with stems down and no spaces showing between florets. (Broccoli can be arranged on platter up to 3 hours before serving, covered with plastic wrap, and refrigerated until needed.)

2. In a small bowl, combine reserved cooking liquid, lemon juice, honey, ginger, shallots, salt, and pepper; stir with fork or small whisk. Add olive oil and whisk until dressing is well blended. Spoon dressing over florets just before serving and garnish with lemon zest.

Per Serving: Cal. 94   Carb. 15 gm   Chol. 0 mg
              Fat 3 gm   Prot. 7 gm   Sod. 138 mg

Cauliflower Salad with Caper-Basil Vinaigrette

[Insalata di Cavolfiore]

SERVES 6

Adding the warm cauliflower to the dressing will bring out the full flavor of this salad. To keep the basil and parsley from wilting, add to the salad just before serving.

1 large head cauliflower (about 2¼ pounds)	1 tablespoon extra virgin olive oil
1 teaspoon minced garlic	3 tablespoons nonpareil capers, thoroughly rinsed and well drained
2 tablespoons white wine vinegar	
½ teaspoon coarse salt	¼ cup minced fresh basil
½ teaspoon crushed red pepper flakes	2 tablespoons minced Italian flat-leaf parsley

1. Remove florets from cauliflower, leaving about ½ inch of stems. Cut florets into 1-inch pieces. Wash in cold water and drain.
2. Put cauliflower florets in a steamer set into a 5-quart saucepan containing 1 inch of water. Cook, covered, over medium-high heat until tender, about 7 minutes. Remove steamer and let cauliflower cool slightly. Measure out 3 tablespoons of liquid from bottom of saucepan and reserve for dressing.
3. In a deep bowl, combine reserved cooking liquid, garlic, vinegar, salt, and pepper flakes. Stir with fork or whisk. Add olive oil and whisk until dressing is well blended; stir in capers. Add warm cauliflower to dressing; toss gently. Cover with plastic wrap and marinate at room temperature for at least 1 hour. Add basil and parsley; gently toss once again. Transfer to platter and serve.

Per Serving: Cal. 45   Carb. 5 gm   Chol. 0 mg
               Fat 2 gm   Prot. 2 gm   Sod. 246 mg

Mixed Green Salad with Fresh Tomato-Herb Dressing

[Insalata Mista alla Anna]

SERVES 6

The dressing for this salad can be made up to 2 hours ahead of time. This dressing is also excellent over 1½ pounds of cooked green beans, which have cooled to room temperature before tossing.

1 medium well-ripened round tomato (about 4 ounces), blanched and peeled (see page 126 for technique), cut into 1-inch pieces, with juice included

¼ cup sliced scallions, cut into ½-inch lengths

6 large fresh basil leaves

6 large fresh mint leaves

½ teaspoon sugar

½ teaspoon coarse salt

½ teaspoon freshly milled black pepper

1 tablespoon red wine vinegar

2 teaspoons extra virgin olive oil

1 small head romaine lettuce, bottom trimmed and leaves washed and spun dry before tearing into bite-size pieces, to make 4 cups

1 small bunch arugula, stems discarded, thoroughly washed, spun dry, and cut into bite-size pieces, to make 2 cups

1 small bunch watercress, coarse stems discarded, rinsed, spun dry, and cut into 2-inch lengths, to make 2 cups

1 large head Belgian endive (3 ounces), halved lengthwise, cored, washed, spun dry, and sliced crosswise into ½-inch widths

½ cup thinly sliced celery, strings removed before slicing

1. Put tomato, scallions, basil, mint, sugar, salt, pepper, vinegar, and olive oil in food processor. Process by pulsing with quick on/off action until tomato, scallions, and herbs are finely minced and dressing has a smooth creamy consistency.

2. In a salad bowl, combine romaine, arugula, watercress, endive, and celery. Spoon dressing over salad, toss gently, and serve.

Per Serving: Cal. 34   Carb. 4 gm   Chol. 0 mg
              Fat 2 gm   Prot. 2 gm   Sod. 146 mg

Lentil Salad with Orange-Mint Dressing

[Insalata di Lenticchie]

SERVES 8

This salad is surprisingly light and full of pleasing textures. The lentils take on the sweetness of the orange and mint dressing while the carrots and celery add crunch.

2 cups lentils, picked over to remove any foreign matter, rinsed, and drained

2 large bay leaves

½ cup diced peeled carrots (¼-inch dice)

½ cup diced celery (¼-inch dice), strings removed before dicing

½ cup minced red onion

1 tablespoon finely grated zest of navel orange

⅓ cup strained fresh orange juice

1 teaspoon Dijon-style mustard

4 teaspoons white wine vinegar

½ teaspoon coarse salt

½ teaspoon freshly milled black pepper

1 tablespoon extra virgin olive oil

2 tablespoons minced fresh mint

¼ cup minced Italian flat-leaf parsley

8 large romaine lettuce leaves, washed and trimmed, for garnish

1. Put lentils, bay leaves, and 6 cups water in a 5-quart saucepan. Cover pot and bring to a boil over medium heat. Turn heat to low and cook, partially covered, until lentils are tender, about 25 to 30 minutes. (Watch carefully so that lentils do not overcook.) Drain

in strainer, rinse under cold water, and thoroughly drain again; discard bay leaves. Transfer to a deep bowl and add carrots, celery, and onion; toss lightly to combine.

2. In a small bowl, combine orange zest, orange juice, mustard, vinegar, salt, and pepper. Stir with fork or whisk. Add olive oil and whisk until dressing is well blended. Drizzle dressing over lentil mixture and toss gently. Cover with plastic wrap and refrigerate until slightly chilled, about 30 minutes. (Salad can be prepared up to 3 hours before serving. Remove from refrigerator one-half hour before serving.) Add mint and parsley just before serving; toss once again.

3. On a large platter, arrange romaine leaves in an outside border. Spoon lentil salad in center and serve.

Per Serving: Cal. 196   Carb. 31 gm   Chol. 0 mg
                Fat 2 gm   Prot. 14 gm   Sod. 123 mg

Orange and Cucumber Salad with Anise Seed Dressing

[Insalata d'Aranci e Cetriolo]

SERVES 4

Here is a good refreshing winter salad when large firm navel oranges are available.

4 large navel oranges (about 2½ pounds)
1 medium European-style seedless cucumber (about 9 ounces), washed, trimmed, skin scored with a fork, and sliced into ¼-inch rounds
½ teaspoon crushed anise seed
1 tablespoon minced red onion
1 tablespoon white wine vinegar

¼ teaspoon coarse salt
⅛ teaspoon freshly milled white pepper
2 teaspoons extra virgin olive oil
1 tablespoon minced fresh mint
6 short sprigs fresh mint, for garnish

1. Cut a slice from top and bottom of each orange to expose the fruit. Peel the oranges and remove all the white membrane with a vegetable peeler. Slice crosswise into ¼-inch rounds. Place orange sections in a strainer set over a bowl to drain thoroughly for at least 30 minutes; reserve ¼ cup juice for dressing.
2. On a flat round platter, arrange orange slices and cucumbers in a circular pattern, with slices slightly overlapping. (Salad can be prepared up to 3 hours ahead. Cover with plastic wrap and refrigerate until ready to serve. Spoon dressing over salad just before serving.)
3. In a small bowl, put reserved juice, anise seed, onion, vinegar, salt, and pepper. Stir with fork or small whisk. Add olive oil and whisk until dressing is well blended. Stir in mint. Spoon dressing over salad, garnish with fresh mint, and serve.

Per Serving: Cal. 121 Carb. 25 gm Chol. 0 mg
Fat 2 gm Prot. 2 gm Sod. 94 mg

Baby Spinach, Walnut, and Goat Cheese Salad

[Insalata di Spinaci con Noce e Formaggio Caprino]

SERVES 6

If small clusters of baby spinach are unavailable, you may substitute mesclun, which is simply a generic name for an assortment of wild or baby lettuces.

⅓ cup walnuts, lightly toasted, cooled to room temperature, and coarsely chopped

8 cups baby spinach leaves (or mixed baby greens), washed and spun dry in salad spinner

¼ cup snipped Italian parsley leaves

1 tablespoon minced fresh oregano or 1 teaspoon dried oregano

½ teaspoon coarse salt

½ teaspoon freshly milled white pepper

½ teaspoon sugar

2 tablespoons white wine vinegar

1 tablespoon plus 1 teaspoon extra virgin olive oil

1 ounce mild goat's milk cheese, crumbled (⅓ cup)

1. In a salad bowl, combine walnuts, spinach leaves, parsley, and oregano.
2. Put salt, pepper, sugar, and vinegar in a small bowl. Stir with fork or whisk. Add olive oil and whisk until dressing is well blended. Toss dressing with salad. Sprinkle crumbled goat cheese on top and toss lightly once again before serving.

Per Serving: Cal. 90   Carb. 4 gm   Chol. 7 mg
Fat 6 gm   Prot. 4 gm   Sod. 216 mg

Tomato and Ricotta Salata Salad with Basil-Oil Dressing

[Insalata di Pomodoro con Ricotta Salata]

SERVES 6

In late summer, when New Jersey beefsteak tomatoes are at the peak of the season, I serve this salad at least once a week. Semisoft ricotta salata is available in many supermarkets or Italian specialty shops. Basil oil is an infused mixture of extra virgin olive oil and basil available in gourmet shops and many supermarkets. If basil oil is unavailable, substitute extra virgin olive oil and increase the snipped basil to 3 tablespoons.

5 large well-ripened round tomatoes (about 2½ pounds) washed, dried, and cored	1 tablespoon basil oil
	1 teaspoon freshly milled black pepper
1½ ounces ricotta salata cheese (semisoft variety)	2 tablespoons snipped fresh basil leaves

1. Slice off about ½ inch from tops and bottoms of tomatoes; discard tops and bottoms. Slice each tomato into ½-inch rounds. Arrange slices in a single layer on large platter.
2. Using a hand-held grater with coarse holes, grate the ricotta salata over the tomato slices. Drizzle basil oil over surface and season with pepper. Sprinkle basil on top and serve.

Per Serving: Cal. 78   Carb. 9 gm   Chol. 6 mg
              Fat 4 gm   Prot. 3 gm   Sod. 136 mg

Vegetable Medley with Balsamic Dressing

[Insalata Vegetarina]

SERVES 4

This colorful medley of vegetables with a slightly tart dressing is a pleasing partner to Polenta with Leeks and Sage (page 62). The vegetables should all be cut into thin julienne strips about ½ inch wide by 2 inches long so they will cook uniformly.

¾ cup Vegetable Broth, preferably homemade (page 4), or low-sodium canned

1 cup loosely packed julienned scallions

3 medium peeled carrots (6 ounces) cut into julienne strips

1 large red bell pepper (8 ounces), halved, cored, deribbed, and cut into julienne strips

2 small zucchini (8 ounces), scrubbed, trimmed, and cut into julienne strips

2 small yellow squash

(8 ounces), washed, trimmed, and cut into julienne strips

½ teaspoon sugar

¼ teaspoon coarse salt

¼ teaspoon freshly milled white pepper

2 tablespoons balsamic vinegar

2 teaspoons extra virgin olive oil

1½ teaspoons minced fresh oregano or ½ teaspoon dried oregano

1 medium head radicchio (about 6 ounces), leaves separated, washed, and spun dry

1. Heat broth over medium-high heat in a 12-inch nonstick skillet. Add scallions, carrots, and bell pepper. Turn heat to low and cook, partially covered, until barely tender, about 1 minute. Add zucchini

and yellow squash; cook until all the vegetables are tender-crisp, about 2 minutes. Transfer vegetables to a strainer set over a bowl to drain thoroughly, pressing with the back of a spoon until all the liquid is exuded. Transfer vegetables to a deep bowl. Measure out 2 tablespoons of broth from bottom of bowl and reserve for dressing. Discard remaining broth or reserve for another use.

2. In a small bowl, combine reserved broth, sugar, salt, pepper, and vinegar. Stir with fork or whisk. Add olive oil and whisk until dressing is blended; stir in oregano. Pour dressing over vegetables and toss gently. Cover with plastic wrap and refrigerate until chilled, about 1 hour. (Salad can be made up to 4 hours before serving.)

3. On a flat round platter, arrange radicchio leaves in an outside border. Spoon vegetable salad in center and serve.

Per Serving: Cal. 93   Carb. 16 gm   Chol. 0 mg
              Fat 3 gm   Prot. 3 gm   Sod. 119 mg

Zucchini and Roasted Pepper Salad

[Insalata di Zucchini e Pepe Arrostiti]

SERVES 6

If bright, firm orange bell peppers are unavailable, you may substitute yellow or red bells peppers for this salad.

5 small zucchini (about 1¼ pounds)

3 large, firm orange bell peppers (1½ pounds), roasted and peeled (see page 125 for technique), sliced lengthwise into ½-inch strips

1 teaspoon minced garlic

2 teaspoons minced fresh oregano or ½ teaspoon dried oregano

1 tablespoon balsamic vinegar

½ teaspoon coarse salt

½ teaspoon freshly milled black pepper

2 teaspoons extra virgin olive oil

3 tablespoons minced Italian flat-leaf parsley, for garnish

1. Scrub zucchini under cold running water until the skins feel clean and smooth. Put zucchini in a steamer set into a 4-quart saucepan containing 1 inch of water. Cook, covered, over medium-high heat, until barely tender, about 3 minutes. Remove steamer and let zucchini cool to room temperature. Spoon out 3 tablespoons of the cooking liquid from bottom of saucepan and reserve for dressing. Trim ends of zucchini and slice in half lengthwise. Slice each half into strips 2½ inches long and ½ inch wide. Transfer to shallow bowl and combine with roasted peppers.

2. Place reserved cooking liquid, garlic, oregano, vinegar, salt, and pepper in a small bowl. Stir with fork or small whisk. Add olive oil

and whisk until dressing is well blended. Toss dressing with zucchini and roasted peppers. Garnish with minced parsley and serve.

Per Serving: Cal. 54   Carb. 9 gm   Chol. 0 mg
              Fat 2 gm   Prot. 2 gm   Sod. 128 mg

Pizza and Focaccia

Introduction

Pizza has become one of the most popular foods in the world today. It is as much fun to make as it is to eat. Pizza is a simple food, made just like bread, with flour, yeast, and water.

In this chapter, you will find the classic pizza dough that can be shaped into 4 small rounds, a large thin round, or the thick-crusted Sicilian-style pizza that requires a double rising. Another approach is the quick-rise method, incorporating a little cornmeal, which yields a crisper crust. This dough is ready in 20 minutes and may be shaped into small rounds or one large thin round. The toppings range from traditional tomato sauce and mozzarella to artichoke and raisin, white bean tomato-basil, and other more exotic vegetable combinations.

As every pizza connoisseur knows, the secret to a great pizza is the crust. Since the preferences range from thin and crispy to thick and bread-like, a variety of choices are offered. If you are a serious pizza maker, I would suggest that you purchase a large 18-inch-square pizza stone about ½ inch thick and follow the manufacturer's directions for using it. This will produce a crust like those traditionally baked in brick ovens. You should also have a wooden pizza peel, or a rimless baking sheet that is dusted with cornmeal to allow the pizza to slide off the paddle or baking sheet onto the stone. However, the home baker can still make exceptional pizza with either a 14-inch-round pizza pan or a large 14 × 17-inch cookie sheet set on the lowest shelf of a preheated oven according to the temperature specified in each recipe.

Focaccia is a rustic flat bread, similar to pizza but lighter in texture because the dough has two risings. This famed flat bread is delicious served with soup, vegetable entrées, salads, or even alone as an appetizer or snack food. It can be eaten hot from the oven or at room temperature. In addition to the flat bread recipes, there is a doubled-crusted Neapolitan endive pie that only requires one rising of the focaccia dough and can be served as an accompaniment to any soup, or on its own for a great lunch.

Once you've made your own pizza or focaccia, you'll realize that while you've tried the rest, you've finally found the best!

Pizza Dough

ENOUGH DOUGH FOR 1 LARGE 14-INCH ROUND OR
FOUR 7-INCH ROUND PIZZAS, 8 SLICES

½ teaspoon sugar
¾ cup lukewarm water,
    105°F. to 115°F.
1 package (¼ ounce) active
    dry yeast

2 teaspoons olive oil
2 to 2¼ cups bread flour or
    unbleached all-purpose
    flour
½ teaspoon coarse salt

In a 2-cup glass measure, stir sugar into water. Sprinkle yeast over water and stir briefly until completely dissolved. Set aside until foamy, about 5 minutes. Add olive oil and whisk to combine.

FOOD PROCESSOR METHOD: Place 2 cups flour and the salt in food processor; process for 15 seconds to combine. With machine running, slowly pour dissolved yeast mixture through feed tube and process for 50 seconds. (Dough will form a mass and is kneaded by spinning in machine for this period of time.) At this point, dough should feel slightly sticky. If dough feels wet, gradually add remaining ¼ cup flour, 1 tablespoon at a time, process for 5 seconds after each addition, until dough reaches desired consistency. Transfer dough to lightly floured surface and knead until smooth and satiny, about 2 minutes. Shape dough into a ball.

ELECTRIC MIXER METHOD: Put 1½ cups flour and salt in bowl of electric mixer fitted with flat paddle attachment; run machine at low speed for 20 seconds to combine. Add yeast mixture and run machine on medium speed until dough starts to pull together in a sticky mass. Scrape dough from paddle attachment into bowl. Remove paddle attachment and insert dough hook. Add additional flour, 2 tablespoons at a time, and run machine on medium speed until dough is kneaded into a soft mass that pulls away from sides of bowl, about 3 minutes.

Transfer dough to a lightly floured surface and knead until smooth and satiny, about 5 minutes. Shape dough into a ball.

HAND METHOD: Place 1¼ cups flour and salt in a deep bowl; stir to combine. Stir in yeast mixture and beat with wooden spoon until blended. Gradually stir in additional flour, ¼ cup at a time, until mixture forms a ball that cleans the sides of bowl. Transfer to a lightly floured surface and knead dough, adding additional flour as needed, until smooth and satiny, about 8 to 10 minutes. Shape dough into a ball.

Lightly grease bottom and sides of a deep 2-quart bowl with olive oil cooking spray. Place dough in greased bowl, turning ball to coat entire surface with oil. Cover tightly with plastic wrap and place a dish towel over surface. Let rise in draft-free area until doubled in size, about 55 to 60 minutes. Punch risen dough down in center. Transfer to a lightly floured surface and knead briefly. Reshape into 1 ball and lightly dust with flour for one 14-inch round pizza, or reshape into 4 small round balls if making four 7-inch pizzas. Cover with dish towel and let dough rest on a well-floured board for about 12 minutes, so gluten mesh will relax a little, making it easier to shape or roll. Dough is now ready to be shaped, topped, and cooked.

Per Slice:	Cal. 139	Carb. 25 gm	Chol. 0 mg
	Fat 2 gm	Prot. 4 gm	Sod. 93 mg

Broccoli with Caramelized Onion Pizza

[Pizza di Broccoli e Cipolla]

❖

MAKES ONE 14-INCH ROUND PIZZA, 8 SLICES

This pizza is for broccoli lovers. The caramelized onion adds a slightly sweet flavor, while the hot pepper flakes add an extra little zip.

Pizza Dough (page 155)

2 cups thinly sliced Spanish or Texas White onions

⅔ cup Vegetable Broth, preferably homemade (page 4), or low-sodium canned

4 cups bite-size pieces broccoli florets with ¼ inch of stems included, washed and drained

1½ teaspoons cornmeal for dusting pan

1 tablespoon extra virgin olive oil

½ teaspoon coarse salt

½ teaspoon crushed red pepper flakes

1½ tablespoons minced fresh sage or 1½ teaspoons crumbled dried sage

⅓ cup well-packed freshly grated imported Parmesan cheese

1. Prepare pizza dough.
2. Adjust oven rack to lowest position in oven and preheat to 450°F. for 20 minutes.
3. In a 10-inch nonstick skillet, cook onions in vegetable broth over medium heat, stirring frequently, until onions start to turn a deep golden color and no liquid is left in bottom of pan, about 7 to 8 minutes.
4. Put broccoli florets in a steamer set into a 5-quart saucepan con-

taining 1 inch of water. Cook, covered, over medium heat until barely tender, about 4 minutes. Remove steamer and let vegetables cool to room temperature.

5. Lightly spray a 14-inch round pizza pan with olive oil cooking spray and dust with cornmeal.
6. Place ball of dough on well-floured work surface. With the palm of your hand, flatten dough into a round disk. Flip dough over. Use a rolling pin to shape dough into a 14-inch circle, turning and stretching it gently as you roll, and adding more flour to work surface if necessary to prevent sticking. Transfer dough to prepared pan.
7. Distribute onions evenly over surface to within ½ inch of outside rim of dough. Arrange broccoli florets over onions. Drizzle olive oil over florets. Sprinkle salt, pepper flakes, sage, and Parmesan cheese over florets.
8. Bake until edges are golden brown and bottom crust is crisp, about 20 to 25 minutes. Transfer to cutting board and let cool slightly before cutting into 8 wedges.

Per Slice: Cal. 205   Carb. 34 gm   Chol. 2 mg
               Fat 5 gm   Prot. 8 gm   Sod. 221 mg

Traditional Pizza

[Pizza Tradizionale]

MAKES FOUR 7-INCH ROUND PIZZAS, 8 SLICES

Everyone loves the traditional pizza with a topping of tomato sauce, mozzarella, and dried oregano. This is a much lower-fat version than one you would buy at your local pizzeria.

1 ¼ cups Tomato-Basil Sauce
       (page 24)
       Pizza Dough (page 155)
   3   teaspoons cornmeal for
       dusting pans

   1   teaspoon dried oregano
   2   ounces part-skim
       mozzarella cheese, grated
       to make ½ cup

1. Prepare sauce 1 hour before making dough.
2. Prepare pizza dough.
3. Adjust one oven rack to lowest position in oven. Adjust second rack
   to center of oven and preheat to 450°F. for 20 minutes. Lightly
   grease two 14 × 17-inch cookie sheets with olive oil cooking spray
   and dust each pan with 1½ teaspoons cornmeal.
4. Place 1 ball of dough on well-floured work surface (keep remaining
   dough covered with towel). With the palm of your hand, flatten
   dough into a round disk. Flip dough over and use fingertips or
   rolling pin to shape or roll dough into a 7-inch circle, turning and
   stretching it gently as you roll, adding more flour to work surface if
   necessary to prevent sticking. Transfer dough to prepared pan. Repeat with remaining dough, placing 2 circles on each pan and spacing them 3 inches apart.
5. Spread ¼ cup plus 1 tablespoon sauce over each round to within
   ½ inch of outside rim of dough. Sprinkle ¼ teaspoon oregano and
   2 tablespoons mozzarella over each surface.
6. Bake until edges are golden brown and bottom crust is crisp, about
   15 to 20 minutes, switching the position of pans after baking
   10 minutes. Transfer to cutting board and let cool slightly before
   cutting each pizza in half to serve.

Per Slice: Cal. 176   Carb. 29 gm   Chol. 3 mg
                Fat 4 gm   Prot. 6 gm   Sod. 201 mg

Thick-Crusted Pizza Palermo Style

[Sfunciuni alla Palermitano]

MAKES ONE 14-INCH ROUND PIZZA, 8 SLICES

The secret to this light-textured thick crust is its two risings, the first in the bowl and the second in the pan. Fans of this type of crust may use it for any of the pizza toppings in this chapter.

Pizza Dough (page 155)
1½ teaspoons cornmeal (for dusting pan)
1 tablespoon extra virgin olive oil
⅔ cup finely chopped onion
2½ tablespoons tomato paste
¾ cup water
½ teaspoon coarse salt
½ teaspoon freshly milled black pepper
½ cup coarsely chopped dark raisins

1 can (13.5 ounces) whole artichoke hearts, rinsed, drained, halved, and sliced into ¼-inch wedges
⅓ cup coarsely grated mellow Asiago or mild provolone cheese
¼ cup dry bread crumbs, lightly toasted
¼ cup minced Italian flat-leaf parsley

1. Prepare pizza dough.
2. Lightly grease a 14-inch round pizza pan with olive oil cooking spray and dust with cornmeal.
3. In a 10-inch nonstick skillet, heat olive oil over low heat. Add onion and cook, stirring frequently, until lightly golden, about 5 minutes.
4. Dissolve tomato paste in water. Add to skillet, season with salt and pepper; cook sauce over medium heat, stirring frequently, for 5 min-

utes. Stir in raisins and cook for an additional minute. Set sauce aside.

5. Place ball of dough on well-floured work surface. With the palm of your hands, flatten dough into a round disk. Flip dough over. Use a rolling pin to shape dough into a 14-inch circle, turning and stretching it gently as you roll, adding more flour to work surface if necessary to prevent sticking. Transfer dough to prepared pan. Loosely cover pan with a towel and let dough rise in warm place for an additional 50 minutes.

6. Adjust oven rack to lowest position in oven and preheat to 450°F. for 20 minutes.

7. Arrange artichoke wedges over pizza surface to within ½ inch of outside rim of dough. Spoon sauce over surface and sprinkle with cheese and bread crumbs.

8. Bake until edges are golden brown and bottom crust is crisp, about 25 to 30 minutes. Transfer to cutting board and garnish with parsley. Let cool slightly before cutting into 8 wedges.

Per Slice:	Cal. 216	Carb. 37 gm	Chol. 3 mg
	Fat 4 gm	Prot. 7 gm	Sod. 292 mg

White Bean, Tomato, and Basil Pizza

[Pizza con Fagioli e Pomodoro]

MAKES ONE 14-INCH ROUND PIZZA, 8 SLICES

The basil-scented white beans give a creamy texture to the pizza, while the tomatoes and mozzarella add an adorning touch to this Tuscan specialty.

〜〜

Pizza dough (page 155)
2 teaspoons olive oil
⅔ cup minced onion
2 teaspoons minced garlic
1 can (19 ounces) cannellini (white kidney) beans, rinsed and well drained
¾ cup dry white wine
1 tablespoon minced fresh basil or 1 teaspoon dried basil
1½ teaspoons cornmeal for dusting pan

2 large well-ripened round tomatoes (about 1 pound), cored, ends trimmed, and sliced into ¼-inch rounds
½ teaspoon coarse salt
½ teaspoon freshly milled black pepper
1½ ounces part-skim mozzarella, grated to make ⅓ cup

1. Prepare pizza dough.
2. Adjust oven rack to lowest position in oven and preheat to 450°F. for 20 minutes.
3. In a 10-inch nonstick skillet, heat olive oil over low heat. Add onion and sauté, stirring frequently until soft, about 4 minutes. Stir in garlic and cook an additional 30 seconds. Stir in beans and wine. Cook the mixture, stirring frequently, until beans are very soft and the liquid in the pan is reduced to half, about 7 minutes. Remove from heat. With the back of a wooden spoon, mash bean mixture into a paste. Stir in basil and remove from heat.
4. Lightly spray a 14-inch round pizza pan with olive oil cooking spray and dust with cornmeal.
5. Place ball of dough on well-floured work surface. With the palm of your hand, flatten dough into a round disk. Flip dough over. Use a rolling pin to shape dough into a 14-inch circle, turning and stretching it gently as you roll, adding more flour to work surface if necessary to prevent sticking. Transfer dough to prepared pan.
6. Spread bean mixture over surface to within ½ inch of outside rim of dough. Arrange tomatoes in a circular pattern on top. (You may have to slice a couple in half to fit in center.) Sprinkle salt and pepper over surface. Sprinkle cheese over tomato slices.
7. Bake until edges are golden brown and bottom crust is crisp, about 20 to 25 minutes. Transfer to cutting board and let cool slightly before cutting into 8 wedges.

~~~~~~

Per Slice: Cal. 240   Carb. 37 gm   Chol. 3 mg
               Fat 4 gm   Prot. 10 gm   Sod. 299 mg

Quick-Rise Cornmeal Pizza Dough

❖

MAKES ENOUGH DOUGH FOR ONE LARGE 14-INCH ROUND
OR FOUR 7-INCH ROUND PIZZAS, 8 SLICES

*A quick and easy pizza dough to make with the added crunch of cornmeal.
Using quick-acting active dry yeast, this dough is ready for any of the
recommended toppings in less than 20 minutes.*

2   to 2½ cups bread flour or
    unbleached all-purpose
    flour
½   cup cornmeal
1   package (¼ ounce) quick-
    acting active dry yeast,
    preferably Fleischmann's
    RapidRise

2   teaspoons sugar
½   teaspoon coarse salt
1   tablespoon olive oil
1   cup hot tap water (125° to
    130°F.)

FOOD PROCESSOR METHOD: Place 2 cups of the flour, the cornmeal,
yeast, sugar, and salt in food processor fitted with metal blade; process
for 30 seconds to combine. With machine running, gradually pour olive
oil and hot tap water in feed tube. Run machine until dough forms a
ball, about 50 seconds. (Dough will form a mass and is kneaded by
spinning in machine for this period of time.) At this point, dough
should feel slightly sticky. If dough feels wet, gradually add reserved
flour, 1 tablespoon at a time; process for 5 seconds after each addition
until dough reaches desired consistency. Transfer dough to lightly
floured surface and knead until smooth and satiny, about 2 minutes.

Shape into a ball and dust lightly with flour. Cover with towel and let rest for 10 minutes. (This rest period replaces the first rising.) Shape, top, and bake as directed.

ELECTRIC MIXER METHOD: Place 1¾ cups of the flour, the cornmeal, yeast, sugar, and salt in bowl of electric mixer fitted with flat paddle attachment. Run machine at low speed for 20 seconds to combine. Add olive oil and hot tap water. Run machine on medium speed until dough starts to pull together in a sticky mass. Scrape dough from paddle attachment into bowl. Remove paddle attachment and insert dough hook. Add additional flour, 2 tablespoons at a time, and run machine on medium speed until dough is kneaded into a soft mass that pulls away from sides of bowl, about 3 minutes. Transfer dough to a lightly floured surface and knead until smooth and satiny, about 5 minutes. Shape into a ball and dust lightly with flour. Cover with towel and let rest for 10 minutes. (This rest period replaces the first rising.) Shape, top, and bake as directed.

HAND METHOD: In a large bowl, combine 1½ cups of flour, the cornmeal, yeast, sugar, and salt. Stir in olive oil and hot tap water. Gradually stir in additional flour, ¼ cup at a time, until mixture forms a ball that cleans the sides of bowl. Transfer to well-floured surface and knead, adding additional flour as needed, until dough is smooth and satiny, about 5 to 6 minutes. Cover with towel and let rest for 10 minutes. (This rest period replaces the first rising.) Shape, top, and bake as directed.

Per Slice: Cal. 181 Carb. 35 gm Chol. 0 mg
            Fat 2 gm Prot. 5 gm Sod. 93 mg

Cornmeal Pizzas with Spinach and Roasted Peppers

[Pizzette con Spinaci e Pepe Arrostiti]

❖

MAKES FOUR 7-INCH PIZZAS, 8 SLICES

Be sure to prepare the topping before making the dough for these pizzas. If you don't have time to roast peppers, substitute two 7-ounce jars roasted peppers. These simple-to-prepare pizzas can be ready to serve in less than 1 hour from start to finish.

1	bag (10 ounces) fresh spinach leaves		Quick-Rise Cornmeal Pizza Dough (page 163)
2	teaspoons extra virgin olive oil	2	large red bell peppers (1 pound), roasted and peeled (see page 125 for technique), sliced lengthwise into ¼-inch strips
1½	tablespoons minced garlic		
1½	teaspoons minced fresh rosemary or ½ teaspoon chopped dried rosemary		
¼	teaspoon coarse salt	6	tablespoons coarsely grated Asiago cheese
½	teaspoon freshly milled black pepper		
3	teaspoons cornmeal for dusting pans		

1. Discard stems from spinach. Wash leaves several times in tepid water to remove grit. Remove spinach from final rinse water and place in a deep colander. Place colander in sink. Bring 4 cups water to a boil. Pour boiling water over spinach until it is wilted, about 20 seconds. Refresh under cold water, drain thoroughly, and squeeze out excess water with your hands. Coarsely chop spinach.
2. In a 10-inch nonstick skillet, heat olive oil over low heat. Add garlic

and sauté, stirring constantly, until lightly golden, about 30 seconds. Stir in spinach and cook, tossing, until combined with garlic mixture, about 20 seconds. Stir in rosemary, season with salt and pepper, and remove from heat; set aside.

3. Adjust one oven rack to lowest position in oven. Adjust second rack to center of oven and preheat to 425°F. for 20 minutes. Lightly grease two 14 × 17-inch cookie sheets with olive oil cooking spray. Dust each pan with 1½ teaspoons cornmeal; set aside.

4. Make single recipe of cornmeal pizza. After dough has rested for 10 minutes, divide it into 4 equal pieces. Place 1 piece of dough on a lightly floured work surface, keeping remaining dough covered with towel. With the palm of your hand, flatten dough into a round disk. Flip dough over and use fingertips or rolling pin to shape or roll into a 7-inch circle, turning and stretching it gently as you roll, adding more flour to work surface if necessary to prevent sticking. Transfer dough to prepared pan. Repeat with remaining dough, placing 2 circles on each pan and spacing them 3 inches apart.

5. Spoon spinach mixture over each round to within ¼ inch of outside rim of dough. Place strips of roasted peppers over spinach mixture. Sprinkle 1½ tablespoons grated cheese over each pizza.

6. Bake until bottoms and edges of crust are golden brown, about 15 to 20 minutes, switching the position of the baking sheets after 10 minutes. Transfer to cutting board and let cool slightly before cutting each pizza in half to serve.

Per Slice:	Cal. 232	Carb. 40 gm	Chol. 3 mg
	Fat 5 gm	Prot. 7 gm	Sod. 199 mg

Cornmeal Pizza with Zucchini and Mushrooms

[Pizza con Zucchini e Funghi]

▩

MAKES ONE 14-INCH ROUND PIZZA, 8 SLICES

For this crispy, truly vegetarian pizza, the dough for the crust should be rolled as thin as possible. If fresh plum tomatoes are unavailable, purchase a 16-ounce can of whole tomatoes. Make the filling before making pizza dough.

2 teaspoons extra virgin olive oil

⅔ cup thinly sliced scallions

6 medium well-ripened plum tomatoes (about 12 ounces), blanched and peeled (see page 126 for technique), coarsely chopped, with juice included

4 small zucchini (about 1 pound), well scrubbed, trimmed, and sliced into ½-inch rounds

12 ounces crimini or white mushrooms, wiped, trimmed, and thinly sliced

½ teaspoon coarse salt

½ teaspoon freshly milled black pepper

1½ teaspoons cornmeal for dusting pan
Quick-Rise Cornmeal Pizza Dough (page 163)

1½ tablespoons minced fresh thyme or 1½ teaspoons dried thyme

¼ cup minced Italian parsley leaves, for garnish

1. In a 12-inch nonstick skillet, heat olive oil over medium heat. Add scallions and sauté, stirring frequently, until lightly golden, about 3 minutes. Stir in tomatoes and juice, turn heat to medium-high, and cook until very little liquid is left in bottom of pan, about 4 minutes. Stir in zucchini and cook, stirring frequently, until barely

tender, about 2 minutes. Stir in mushrooms and cook, stirring frequently, until they start to exude their liquid, about 2 minutes. Turn heat to high and cook, stirring constantly, until no liquid is left in bottom of pan, about 2 minutes; season with salt and pepper, remove from heat, and set aside.

2. Adjust oven rack to lowest position in oven and preheat to 450°F. for 20 minutes. Lightly grease a 14-inch round pizza pan with olive oil cooking spray. Dust pan with cornmeal; set aside.

3. Make single recipe of cornmeal pizza dough. After dough has rested for 10 minutes, place on lightly floured work surface. With the palm of your hands, flatten dough into a round disk. Flip dough over. Using a rolling pin, shape into a 14-inch circle, turning and stretching it gently as you roll, adding more flour to work surface if necessary to prevent sticking. Place on prepared pan. Spoon vegetable mixture over surface to within ½ inch of outside rim of dough. Sprinkle with thyme.

4. Bake until bottom and edges of crust are golden brown, about 20 to 25 minutes. Transfer to cutting board and garnish with parsley. Let cool slightly before cutting pizza into wedges to serve.

Per Slice: Cal. 224   Carb. 41 gm   Chol. 0 mg
            Fat 4 gm   Prot. 7 gm   Sod. 193 mg

Focaccia Dough

❖

For whole-wheat focaccia, see variation at bottom of recipe.

1 teaspoon sugar	1½ tablespoons olive oil
1½ cups lukewarm water, 105°–115°F.	3½ to 4 cups unbleached flour
1 package (¼ ounce) dry yeast	½ teaspoon coarse salt

Stir sugar into water in a 2-cup glass measure. Sprinkle yeast over water and stir briefly until completely dissolved. Set aside until foamy, about 5 minutes. Add olive oil and whisk to combine.

FOOD PROCESSOR METHOD: Place 3½ cups flour and the salt in food processor fitted with metal blade and process for 15 seconds to combine. With machine running, slowly pour dissolved yeast mixture through feed tube and process for 50 seconds. (Dough will form a mass and is kneaded by spinning in machine for this period of time.) At this point, dough should feel slightly sticky. If dough feels wet, gradually add reserved flour, 1 tablespoon at a time; process for 5 seconds after each addition until dough reaches desired consistency. Transfer dough to lightly floured surface and knead until it is smooth and satiny, about 2 minutes. Shape into a ball.

ELECTRIC MIXER METHOD: Put 3 cups flour and salt in bowl of heavy-duty electric mixer fitted with flat paddle attachment; run machine at low speed for 20 seconds to combine. Add yeast mixture and run machine on medium speed until dough starts to pull together in a sticky mass. Scrape dough from paddle attachment into bowl. Remove paddle attachment and insert dough hook. Add additional flour, 3 tablespoons at a time, and run machine on medium speed until dough is kneaded into a soft mass that pulls away from sides of bowl, about 3 minutes. Transfer dough to a lightly floured surface and knead until smooth and satiny, about 5 minutes. Shape dough into a ball.

HAND METHOD: Put 2½ cups flour and salt in a deep bowl; stir to combine. Stir in yeast and beat with wooden spoon until blended. Gradually stir in additional flour, ¼ cup at a time, until mixture forms a ball that cleans the sides of bowl. Transfer to well-floured surface and knead, adding additional flour as needed, until dough is smooth and satiny, about 8 to 10 minutes. Shape into a ball.

Lightly grease bottom and sides of a deep 3-quart bowl with olive oil cooking spray. Place dough in a greased bowl, turning ball to coat entire surface with cooking spray. Cover tightly with plastic wrap and place a dish towel over surface. Let rise in a draft-free area until doubled in size, about 50 to 60 minutes. Punch risen dough down in center. Gently pull the outside edges of dough to center, turn dough over, and shape into a ball once again. Cover tightly with plastic wrap and dish towel; let rise a second time until doubled, about 45 to 50 minutes. Punch risen dough down in center a second time. Transfer to a lightly floured board and knead briefly. Reshape into a ball and dust lightly with flour. Cover with towel, place on lightly floured surface, and let dough rest for at least 20 minutes so gluten will relax and rolling will be easier. Dough is now ready to be rolled, topped, and baked.

VARIATION: To make whole-wheat focaccia, replace 1 cup unbleached flour with 1 cup whole-wheat flour. The first rising will take approximately 90 minutes, and the second rising will take approximately 45 minutes.

Per Slice:	Cal. 64	Carb. 12 gm	Chol. 0 mg
	Fat .86 gm	Prot. 2 gm	Sod. 25 mg

Roasted Garlic and Fresh Herb Focaccia

[Focaccia d'Aglio con Erbe]

❖

MAKES 1 FOCACCIA, YIELDING 30 SLICES

This aromatic focaccia with its subtle flavoring of sweet roasted garlic and fresh herbs is a great partner for any soup or zesty salad. The roasted garlic, combined with broth and extra virgin olive oil, is also an excellent spread on crusty peasant bread, topped off with a little crumbled goat cheese.

Focaccia Dough (page 169)	1½ teaspoons cornmeal for dusting pan
2 whole plump heads of garlic (about 4 ounces)	2 tablespoons minced fresh thyme
½ cup Vegetable Broth, preferably homemade (page 4), or low-sodium canned	2 tablespoons minced fresh sage
1½ tablespoons extra virgin olive oil	1 teaspoon coarse salt
	1 teaspoon freshly milled black pepper

1. Prepare focaccia dough.
2. Adjust oven rack to center of oven and preheat to 400°F.
3. With a sharp knife, cut off and discard the upper third of each garlic head, exposing the cloves. Leave the skin intact below the cut. Place the garlic heads, cut side up, in a deep 3-cup baking dish. Pour vegetable broth over garlic. Cover the dish tightly with heavy-duty aluminum foil and bake until each clove is soft when pierced with the tip of a knife and the skins are lightly browned, about 1 hour. Remove garlic and let cool a little. Strain broth into a shallow bowl. When garlic is cool enough to handle, peel skins and mash cloves into a paste. Stir garlic paste and extra virgin olive oil into broth.

4. Adjust oven rack to lowest position in oven and raise oven temperature to 425°F. Lightly grease a 12 × 17-inch jelly roll pan with olive oil cooking spray and dust with cornmeal.

5. Place dough on well-floured work surface. With the palms of your hands, flatten dough into a rectangular shape. Flip dough over. Using a rolling pin, shape into a rectangle about 12 × 17 inches, turning and stretching dough gently as you roll, adding more flour to work surface if necessary to prevent sticking. Place on prepared pan. With your fingertips, make dimples in dough, leaving indentations that are as deep as ½ inch. Evenly spread garlic mixture over surface to within ½ inch of outside rim of dough. Sprinkle thyme, sage, salt, and pepper over surface.

6. Bake until edges are lightly golden and bottom crust is crisp, about 30 to 40 minutes. Transfer to cutting board, cool slightly, slice into squares, and serve warm or at room temperature.

Per Slice: Cal. 77   Carb. 14 gm   Chol. 0 mg
              Fat 2 gm   Prot. 2 gm   Sod. 75 mg

Gorgonzola, Basil, and Pine Nut Focaccia

[Focaccia alla Genovese]

MAKES 1 FOCACCIA, YIELDING 30 SLICES

Domestic brands of Gorgonzola cheese, available at your local supermarkets, are just as acceptable as the imported brands for this focaccia.

Focaccia Dough (page 169)

1 cup well-packed fresh basil leaves

½ cup well-packed Italian flat-leaf parsley

3½ ounces Gorgonzola cheese, cut into ½-inch chunks

½ cup part-skim ricotta cheese

3 to 5 tablespoons skim milk

⅓ cup pine nuts, lightly toasted

1½ teaspoons cornmeal for dusting pan

2 teaspoons freshly milled black pepper

1. Prepare focaccia dough.
2. Put basil and parsley in food processor; process by pulsing with quick on/off action until chopped. Add Gorgonzola cheese, ricotta, and 3 tablespoons milk. Process until Gorgonzola is finely crumbled and mixture has the consistency of well-beaten whipped cream, about 4 seconds. If mixture is too thick, add remaining milk and process for another second. Add pine nuts and process by pulsing once or twice with quick on/off action until blended.
3. Adjust oven rack to lowest position in oven and preheat to 425°F. for 20 minutes. Lightly grease a 12 × 17-inch jelly roll pan or a 14 × 17-inch cookie sheet with olive oil cooking spray and dust with cornmeal.
4. Place dough on well-floured work surface. With the palms of your hands, flatten dough into a rectangular shape. Flip dough over. Using a rolling pin, shape dough into a rectangle about 12 × 17 inches, turning and stretching it gently as you roll, adding more flour to work surface if necessary to prevent sticking. Place on prepared pan. With your fingertips, make dimples in dough, leaving indentations that are as deep as ½ inch. Evenly spread cheese mixture over surface to within ½ inch of outside rim of dough. Sprinkle with black pepper.
5. Bake for 10 minutes. Lower oven temperature to 375°F. and bake until topping is golden brown and bottom crust is crisp, about 20 to 25 minutes. Transfer to cutting board, cool slightly, slice into squares, and serve warm or at room temperature.

Per Slice:	Cal. 91	Carb. 14 gm	Chol. 4 mg
	Fat 3 gm	Prot. 3 gm	Sod. 71 mg

Neapolitan Curly Endive Pie

[Torta di Scarola Riccia]

16 SLICES

Curly endive is sometimes called curly chicory. If curly endive is unavailable, substitute escarole. My grandson, John Paul, requests this Neapolitan pie for his birthday every year rather than a birthday cake.

Focaccia Dough (page 169)
3 large heads curly endive (about 3 pounds)
1½ tablespoons extra virgin olive oil
1 tablespoon minced garlic
½ cup pitted, finely chopped gaeta or calamata olives

½ teaspoon coarse salt
½ teaspoon crushed red pepper flakes
1 teaspoon cornmeal for dusting pan
1 large egg white, lightly beaten

1. Prepare focaccia dough through first rising. While dough is rising, make endive filling.
2. Discard any wilted or bruised leaves from endive. Separate leaves and trim off about 2 inches of tough bottom ends of greens. Wash greens several times in tepid water to get rid of grit. Place endive in an 8-quart pot. Do not add water; the final rinse water clinging to leaves will be sufficient to steam them. Cook, covered, over high heat, pushing leaves down with wooden spoon once or twice, until stems are tender, about 6 minutes. Transfer to a colander and drain well. Let cool to room temperature. Take ⅓ of the endive, shape into ball, and lightly squeeze with your hands to get rid of some of the

moisture. Coarsely chop and thoroughly squeeze once again to get rid of all the excess moisture. Repeat with remaining endive; set aside.

3. In a 12-inch nonstick skillet, heat olive oil over low heat. Add garlic and sauté until very lightly golden. Add endive and cook over medium heat, stirring frequently, until extremely soft, about 6 minutes. Stir in olives and season with salt and pepper flakes; remove from heat. Cool filling to room temperature.

4. Adjust oven rack to lowest position in oven and preheat to 400°F. for 20 minutes. Lightly grease a 14-inch round pizza pan with olive oil cooking spray and dust with cornmeal.

5. Punch risen dough down in center, transfer to a lightly floured board, and knead briefly. Reshape into 2 balls and dust lightly with flour. Cover with towel, place on lightly floured surface, and let dough rest for at least 15 minutes. Place 1 ball of dough on a well-floured work surface keeping remaining dough covered with towel. With the palms of your hands, flatten dough into an 8-inch circle. Flip dough over. Using a rolling pin, shape into a 14-inch circle, adding more flour to work surface if necessary to prevent sticking. Place dough in prepared pan. Prick surface of dough in several places with fork. Spoon filling on top and spread evenly to within ½ inch of outside rim of dough. Brush rim of dough with lightly beaten egg white. Roll second piece of dough the same as first piece and place on top of filling. Pinch edges of dough together to seal. Prick surface of dough in several places with fork. Brush entire surface of dough with beaten egg white.

6. Bake in preheated oven until surface is golden brown and bottom crust is crisp, about 30 to 40 minutes. Remove from oven and let cool for 15 minutes before slicing into wedges. This pie is also excellent served at room temperature.

Per Slice:	Cal. 156	Carb. 26 gm	Chol. 0 mg
	Fat 4 gm	Prot. 4 gm	Sod. 234 mg

Potato-Rosemary Focaccia

[Focaccia di Patate e Rosmarino]

MAKES 1 FOCACCIA, 30 SLICES

To slice the potatoes paper-thin, you will need a mandoline or hand-held slicing device. This focaccia is an excellent accompaniment to Herbed Split Pea Soup (page 12) or with a glass of chardonnay as an appetizer before dinner.

Focaccia Dough (page 169)
½ cup Vegetable Broth, preferably homemade (page 4), or low-sodium canned
3 tablespoons minced garlic
2 tablespoons finely minced fresh rosemary or 2 teaspoons chopped dried rosemary
1½ tablespoons extra virgin olive oil

1½ teaspoons cornmeal for dusting pan
5 medium red-skinned potatoes (about 1½ pounds), well scrubbed and blotted dry
1 teaspoon coarse salt
1 teaspoon freshly milled black pepper

1. Prepare focaccia dough.
2. While dough is coming to first rising, combine broth, minced garlic, rosemary, and olive oil in a small bowl; cover with plastic wrap and set broth mixture aside.
3. Adjust oven rack to lowest position in oven and preheat to 400°F. for 20 minutes. Lightly grease a 12 × 17-inch jelly roll pan or 14 × 17-inch cookie sheet with olive oil cooking spray and dust with cornmeal.
4. Place dough on well-floured work surface. With the palms of your hands, flatten dough into a rectangular shape. Flip dough over. Us-

ooo

ing a rolling pin, shape into a rectangle about 12 × 17 inches, turning and stretching it gently as you roll, adding more flour to work surface, if necessary, to prevent sticking. Place on prepared pan. Cover dough with towel to keep moist while slicing potatoes.

5. Trim ends of potatoes. With a mandoline or a hand-held slicing device, cut potatoes into ⅛-inch-thick rounds. Arrange sliced potatoes over dough in an overlapping pattern. Whisk broth mixture and brush over potatoes. Sprinkle surface with salt and pepper.

6. Bake in preheated oven until the potatoes are a golden color and bottom crust is crisp, about 50 to 60 minutes. Transfer to cutting board, cool slightly, cut into squares, and serve.

Per Slice:	Cal. 90	Carb. 17 mg	Chol. 0 mg
	Fat 2 gm	Prot. 2 gm	Sod. 76 mg

Desserts

Introduction

Desserts bring back memories of my childhood, when I would be at the lunch table with my classmates and watch them open their bags to see what their mothers had given them. Usually, it was candies, gooey brownies, or iced cupcakes. My bag always had a piece of fruit and sometimes a surprise of a couple of biscotti. If I was invited to friends' homes for dinner, their mothers always said, "Kids, eat all your dinner and you can have dessert." This usually meant a rich, creamy concoction, either an iced chocolate cake or coconut layer cake, or a pie, usually Boston or banana cream. These gustatory celebrations were the prize at the end of the meal.

At my home, the culinary commemoration at the end of a meal was either baked pears, sliced fresh fruit, or a simple spoon dessert like rice pudding or apple bread pudding. When I asked my mother why we didn't have desserts like the ones my friends had, she would offer the following explanation. Desserts are divided into two categories: the ultrarich, for special occasions, and the simple, easy-to-make, uncomplicated ones that end our meals on a light, pleasant note. Of course on holidays the rich, elaborate desserts such as cannoli, sfogliatelle, and cassata displayed in the local pasticceria (pastry shops) were usually purchased for these special occasions, along with trays of fresh fruit and baskets filled with roasted chestnuts and other assorted nuts, always served with espresso coffee.

In teaching lean Italian cooking classes, I am asked by more and more students for desserts with fewer calories and less fat. When I began to think seriously about making them, I wanted to capture the flavoring of the traditional uncomplicated homespun creations my mother used to make. Could I please serious dessert lovers? The results that follow are variations on the treats of my childhood that satisfy one's sweet tooth with less fat, fewer calories, and therefore less guilt. Although they have about one-third to three-quarters less fat than their traditional counterparts, they are sensational desserts—worthy of center-table status.

Apple and Dried Fruit Bread Pudding

[Budino di Pane con Frutti]

SERVES 10

This comforting spiced bread pudding laced with a medley of fruits is excellent served at room temperature or lukewarm with a dollop of fat-free frozen vanilla yogurt on top.

3 cups well-packed 1-inch cubed day-old Italian bread	peeled, halved, cored, and cut into ½-inch cubes
3 cups skim milk	½ cup dark raisins
½ cup unsweetened apple juice	½ cup dried apricots, cut into ½-inch dice
½ cup sugar	¾ cup fat-free egg substitute
4 large Golden Delicious apples (about 1½ pounds),	2 teaspoons vanilla extract
	1 teaspoon ground cinnamon

1. Combine the bread and milk in a large bowl. Set mixture aside to soak for 30 minutes.
2. While bread is soaking, heat apple juice with ¼ cup of sugar in a 12-inch nonstick skillet over medium heat until sugar is dissolved, about 2 minutes. Add apples and cook, stirring frequently, until apples are tender and no liquid is left in bottom of pan. Stir in raisins and apricots and remove from heat. Stir the fruit mixture into the bread mixture and cool to room temperature before adding egg mixture.
3. Adjust oven rack to center of oven and preheat to 325°F. Lightly spray a 9 × 13 × 2-inch ovenproof baking dish with cooking spray; set aside.
4. In a medium bowl, using whisk, beat egg substitute with remaining ¼ cup sugar, vanilla, and cinnamon. Stir into the apple mixture un-

til well combined. Pour mixture into prepared dish. Bake until a knife inserted near center of pudding comes out clean, about 55 to 60 minutes. Remove pudding from oven.

5. Adjust oven rack to 4 inches from heat source and preheat on broil setting. Return pudding to oven and broil until the top is lightly golden, about 1 to 2 minutes. (Watch carefully so it doesn't burn.) Transfer to cooling rack and serve warm or at room temperature.

Per Serving: Cal. 192   Carb. 41 gm   Chol. 1 mg
               Fat .86 gm   Prot. 6 gm   Sod. 153 mg

Silky Chocolate Cream

[Semifreddo di Cioccolata]

SERVES 8

This silky chocolate cream adds a festive finale to any dinner party.

1 tablespoon plus 2 teaspoons unflavored gelatin (1 envelope plus 2 teaspoons)	½ cup sugar
	2 teaspoons pure vanilla extract
2½ cups low-fat (1 percent) milk	1¼ cups fat-free ricotta cheese
⅓ cup unsweetened Dutch-process cocoa	4 teaspoons grated dark semisweet chocolate, for garnish

1. Combine gelatin and 2 cups of the milk in a 1½-quart saucepan. Let stand for 2 minutes to soften gelatin. Stir with whisk over low heat until gelatin is dissolved, about 3 minutes. Transfer to a 1-quart bowl and cool to room temperature. Cover with plastic wrap; place in

refrigerator until mixture jells to the consistency of yogurt, about 60 to 70 minutes.

2. Put remaining ½ cup milk, cocoa, and sugar in a small saucepan; stir with whisk until cocoa is dissolved. Cook over low heat, whisking constantly, until mixture comes to a low boil, about 1 minute. Transfer to bowl, cool to room temperature, and stir in vanilla extract.

3. Put ricotta cheese in food processor and process until smooth, about 20 seconds. Add cocoa mixture and process until well blended and creamy, about 30 seconds. Transfer to a large deep bowl.

4. Place milk-gelatin mixture in electric mixer fitted with whip attachment. Whip on high speed until it has quadrupled in volume and the mixture looks like glossy, stiffly beaten egg whites, about 4 to 5 minutes, stopping machine once to scrape inside of bowl with rubber spatula. Whisk a third of the beaten gelatin mixture into cocoa mixture. With rubber spatula, fold in remaining beaten milk mixture, one-half at a time, into cocoa mixture. Ladle into eight 8-ounce wine goblets and refrigerate until set, about 2 hours. (Dessert can be made a day ahead, covered with plastic wrap, and refrigerated until needed.) Garnish each portion with ½ teaspoon grated chocolate just before serving.

Per Serving: Cal. 144   Carb. 22 gm   Chol. 6 mg
              Fat 2 gm   Prot. 11 gm   Sod. 104 mg

Spiced Honey-Poached Figs

[Fichi con Miele Piccante]

SERVES 4

In Italy fresh figs grow just about everywhere from Tuscany down to Sicily, and are abundant in late summer and early fall. Since the season for fresh figs in this country is very short and these gems are often difficult to find, I have developed this recipe using dried figs so that this dessert can be enjoyed any time. Serve with Orange-Almond Biscotti (page 212).

1½ cups unsweetened apple juice	10 ounces dried Calimyrna figs (about 16), stemmed and halved vertically
3 tablespoons honey, preferably orange blossom	1½ tablespoons julienne strips lemon zest
1 cinnamon stick (3 inches)	
8 whole cloves	

In a 10-inch nonstick skillet, combine the apple juice, honey, cinnamon stick, and cloves. Bring to a boil over medium-low heat and cook syrup for 5 minutes. Add the figs, turn heat to low, and simmer, partially covered, until figs are very soft, about 10 to 15 minutes. With a slotted spoon, transfer figs to a shallow bowl. Bring syrup to a boil over high heat and cook until reduced to about ½ cup. Strain syrup over figs and stir in lemon zest; discard solids. Cool to room temperature before spooning into individual dessert bowls. (Figs may be prepared up to 1 day ahead; cover and refrigerate until needed. Return to room temperature before serving.)

Per Serving:	Cal. 275	Carb. 71 gm	Chol. 0 mg
	Fat 1 gm	Prot. 2 gm	Sod. 12 mg

Melon and Grapes in Mint Syrup

[Macedonia di Meloni ed Uve]

SERVES 6

A simple and refreshing combination of fruits when melons are in season. If you like, you can also substitute Persian or casaba melon for the cantaloupe and honeydew.

¾ cup water
¾ cup white wine
½ cup sugar
3 strips (1 inch each) navel orange zest
¼ cup coarsely chopped fresh mint leaves
½ cup strained fresh orange juice

3 cups honeydew melon balls
3 cups cantaloupe melon balls
1 cup stemmed small seedless red grapes, washed and blotted dry
6 short sprigs fresh mint, for garnish

1. In a 2-quart saucepan, combine the water, wine, sugar, orange zest, and mint leaves. Bring to a boil over medium-low heat and cook, stirring frequently, until the sugar is dissolved, about 4 minutes. Turn heat to low and cook syrup for an additional 3 minutes. Transfer syrup to a strainer set over a bowl; discard solids. Cover syrup with plastic wrap and refrigerate until chilled, about 1 hour.
2. When ready to serve, combine orange juice with syrup. Add the melon balls and grapes; stir gently to combine. Spoon into 6 dessert dishes, preferably glass, garnish each with a sprig of fresh mint, and serve.

Per Serving: Cal. 162   Carb. 37 gm   Chol. 0 mg
               Fat .40 gm   Prot. 1 gm   Sod. 18 mg

Mocha Mousse

[Semifreddo di Moca]

SERVES 8

This velvety, rich-tasting mousse will please anyone who loves the flavors of coffee and chocolate.

1 tablespoon plus 2 teaspoons unflavored gelatin (1 envelope plus 2 teaspoons)

2 cups low-fat (1 percent) milk

1 tablespoon instant espresso powder

2 tablespoons unsweetened Dutch-process cocoa

½ cup hot water

½ cup sugar

2 tablespoons Kahlúa (coffee liqueur)

1 container (8 ounces) fat-free cream cheese, at room temperature, preferably Kraft Philadelphia brand

1. Combine gelatin and milk in a 1½-quart saucepan. Let stand for 2 minutes to soften gelatin. Stir with whisk over low heat until gelatin is dissolved, about 3 minutes. Transfer to a 1-quart bowl and cool to room temperature. Cover with plastic wrap; place in refrigerator until mixture jells to the consistency of yogurt, about 60 to 70 minutes.

2. Dissolve espresso powder and cocoa in hot water in a 2-cup glass measuring cup. Add sugar; stir to dissolve. Let cool to room temperature; stir in coffee liqueur.

3. Spoon cream cheese into food processor and pour in espresso mixture. Process until cream cheese is completely dissolved into espresso mixture, about 50 seconds. Transfer to a large deep bowl.

4. Put milk-gelatin mixture in electric mixer fitted with whip attachment. Whip on high speed until it has quadrupled in volume and the

mixture looks like glossy, stiffly beaten egg whites, about 4 to 5 minutes, stopping machine once to scrape inside of bowl with rubber spatula. Whisk a third of the beaten milk mixture into espresso mixture. With rubber spatula, fold remaining beaten milk mixture, one-half at a time, into espresso mixture. Ladle into eight 8-ounce wine goblets and refrigerate until set, about 1 hour. (Dessert can be made a day ahead, covered with plastic wrap, and refrigerated until needed.)

Per Serving: Cal. 119   Carb. 19 gm   Chol. 5 mg
               Fat .89 gm   Prot. 8 gm   Sod. 181 mg

$\mathcal{N}$ectarines in $\mathcal{R}$ed $\mathcal{W}$ine $\mathcal{S}$yrup

[Pesche Noce con Sciroppo di Vino]

SERVES 6

You can substitute 6 well-ripened peaches for the nectarines in this delightful summer dessert. Blanch peaches in 2 quarts boiling water for 2 minutes and peel before slicing.

1½   cups dry red wine
3   strips (1 inch each) navel orange zest
3   strips (1 inch each) lemon zest
½   cup strained fresh orange juice
½   cup sugar
1   cinnamon stick (3 inches)
6   large, unblemished, well-ripened nectarines (about 2 pounds), washed, dried, halved, pitted, and sliced lengthwise into ½-inch strips
1½   cups fresh blueberries, stemmed, washed, and blotted dry
6   small sprigs fresh mint, for garnish

oo

1. In a 2-quart saucepan, combine wine, orange and lemon zests, orange juice, sugar, and cinnamon stick. Bring to a boil over medium heat and stir once or twice until sugar is completely dissolved, about 5 minutes. Turn heat to low and cook syrup for an additional 5 minutes. Transfer syrup to a deep bowl and cool to room temperature. Place nectarines in bowl and gently stir to combine with syrup. Cover with plastic wrap and refrigerate for at least 4 hours.
2. Using a slotted spoon, transfer nectarines to six 8-ounce wine glasses. Discard orange and lemon zests and cinnamon stick. Spoon syrup over each, arrange blueberries on top, and garnish with mint.

Per Serving: Cal. 205   Carb. 42 gm   Chol. 0 mg
              Fat .81 gm   Prot. 2 gm   Sod. 6 mg

Orange and Strawberry Compote

[Macedonia d'Arancie e Fragole]

SERVES 8

Here is a great conclusion to any meal whenever you can find large, firm navel oranges and fresh strawberries.

2 cups dry red wine
½ cup sugar
2 cinnamon sticks (3 inches each)
6 large navel oranges (about 3 pounds)

1 tablespoon grated orange zest
1 pint strawberries, washed, hulled, and sliced

1. In a 10-inch skillet, combine wine, sugar, and cinnamon sticks. Bring to a boil over medium-low heat. Cook, stirring once or twice, until the syrup is slightly thickened and reduced by half, about 15 minutes. Remove from heat, cool to room temperature, and discard cinnamon sticks.
2. With a sharp knife, cut a small slice from the top and bottom of each orange. With tip of knife, divide orange skin into 6 sections. Peel each section, removing most of the white membrane as you peel. With a vegetable peeler, remove all the remaining white membrane from oranges. Cut out each orange segment, removing its protective membrane as you cut. Slice each large segment in half crosswise and transfer to deep bowl. Pour syrup over oranges and stir in orange zest. Cover with plastic wrap and chill for at least 1 hour.
3. When ready to serve, stir in the sliced strawberries. With a serrated spoon, transfer fruit into eight 6-ounce wine glasses and pour a little syrup over each.

Per Serving: Cal. 152   Carb. 30 gm   Chol. 0 mg
               Fat .24 gm   Prot. 2 gm   Sod. 4 mg

Baked Pears

[Pere al Forno]

SERVES 6

A good late fall or winter dessert to make when Bosc pears are in season.

2	large navel oranges (about 1 pound)	2	cinnamon sticks (3 inches each)
1½	cups dry vermouth	6	medium well-ripened Bosc pears (about 2½ pounds)
1¼	cups water		
¾	cup sugar		

1. With a vegetable peeler, remove six 1-inch strips of orange zest from each orange (12 strips). Squeeze oranges, strain juice, and reserve ½ cup.

2. In a 3-quart saucepan, combine the vermouth, orange zest, reserved juice, water, sugar, and cinnamon sticks. Bring to a boil over medium heat, stirring frequently, until the sugar is dissolved, about 4 minutes. Turn heat to low and simmer the syrup for an additional 6 minutes. Transfer syrup mixture to a 9 × 13 × 2-inch ovenproof baking dish.

3. Adjust oven rack to center of oven and preheat to 375°F.

4. Remove bottom (blossom end) and stem from each pear. Peel pears with a vegetable peeler, and cut in half lengthwise. Using a melon baller, scoop out and remove center core. Cut away the fibrous line leading from core to stem end. To prevent discoloration, place each pear half, as soon as it is prepared, into the baking dish, cut side down. Spoon some syrup and one strip of orange zest over each halved pear. Cover dish tightly with aluminum foil and bake pears in preheated oven for 20 minutes. Remove foil and gently turn pears cut side up. Replace the foil and continue baking until pears are tender when tested with a cake tester, about 20 to 30 minutes longer. Remove from oven, discard foil, and cool to room temperature. Carefully turn pears cut side down in syrup. Cover with plastic wrap and refrigerate for at least 3 hours or overnight.

5. When ready to serve, discard strips of orange zest and cinnamon sticks. Transfer 2 pear halves to each serving plate, cut side down. Starting ½ inch from top, cut pear halves lengthwise at ¼-inch intervals and press gently to fan out slices. Spoon a little syrup over each and serve.

Per Serving: Cal. 273   Carb. 55 gm   Chol. 0 mg
              Fat .74 gm   Prot. 1 gm   Sod. 3 mg

Pineapple Granita with Sambuca

[Granita di Ananasso]

SERVES 6

A light refreshing dessert to serve for any occasion. A couple of Lemon-Walnut Biscotti (page 209) would prove a perfect partner. Granita can be made up to 5 days before serving. After cubes are frozen, pop out one tray at a time, transfer each to a 1-quart size Ziploc plastic storage bag and store in freezer until ready to use. Storing in plastic bags will prevent freezer burns from forming on cubes.

1 can (20 ounces) sliced pineapple in unsweetened pineapple juice
1 cup water
⅓ cup superfine sugar (see Note)

2 tablespoons strained fresh lemon juice
3 tablespoons sambuca or anisette

1. Place pineapple in strainer set over a bowl and drain thoroughly; reserve juice. Slice pineapple into ½-inch pieces and place in food processor. Measure out 1 cup reserved juice and add to pineapple, along with water. Run machine nonstop until pineapple is puréed, about 50 seconds, stopping machine once to scrape down inside of work bowl with plastic spatula. Transfer to a deep bowl. Add sugar and stir vigorously with a whisk until sugar is dissolved into mixture, about 20 seconds. Whisk in lemon juice. Spoon into 2 plastic 16-cube ice cube trays and freeze until firm, about 4 hours or overnight.
2. When ready to serve, pop one tray of frozen cubes into a low wide

bowl. (If you have difficulty removing frozen cubes, run bottom of tray briefly under tepid water to loosen.) Place in food processor and run machine nonstop until no large chunks of ice remain and granita is a smooth texture, about 30 to 40 seconds. Spoon into three 8-ounce wine goblets. Repeat with remaining cubes. Spoon 1 ½ teaspoons sambuca over each portion and serve immediately.

Note: Superfine sugar can be made in food processor. Place ⅓ cup granulated sugar in food processor and run machine nonstop for 30 seconds until texture is superfine.

Per Serving: Cal. 121   Carb. 29 gm   Chol. 0 mg
                  Fat .07 gm   Prot. .40 gm   Sod. 1 mg

Creamy Rice Pudding

[Budino di Riso]

SERVES 6

Rice pudding is one of those comfort foods that is especially satisfying during late fall or winter.

½ cup long-grain rice, preferably Carolina, picked over to remove any dark grains
½ cup water
1 quart skim milk
1 cinnamon stick (3 inches)
½ cup fat-free egg substitute

½ cup sugar
¼ cup coarsely chopped golden raisins
1 teaspoon pure vanilla extract
Ground cinnamon, for garnish

1. Combine rice and water in a heavy 5-quart saucepan. Bring to a boil over medium heat. Cover pan, turn heat to low, and cook until water is completely absorbed, about 4 to 5 minutes. Stir in 3½ cups milk and cinnamon stick. Bring to a boil over medium heat, stirring once or twice. Cover pan, turn heat to low, and cook, stirring occasionally, until rice is tender and most of the milk has been absorbed, about 30 to 35 minutes.
2. While rice is cooking, place egg substitute, sugar, and remaining ½ cup milk in a small bowl; whisk to combine. Stir into rice mixture and continue cooking over low heat, stirring constantly, until pudding is thick and creamy, about 3 minutes. Stir in raisins and remove from heat. Cover pan and let rice rest until raisins are plumped, about 5 minutes. Discard cinnamon stick and stir in vanilla extract. Ladle into dessert bowls and serve at room temperature or chilled. Dust with cinnamon just before serving.

Per Serving: Cal. 221   Carb. 47 gm   Chol. 3 mg
              Fat .44 gm   Prot. 9 gm   Sod. 121 mg

Strawberry Granita

[Granita di Fragole]

SERVES 4

This granita can be made up to 4 days before serving. After cubes are frozen, pop out one tray at a time, transfer each to a 1-quart size Ziploc plastic storage bag and store in freezer until ready to use. Storing in plastic bags will prevent freezer burns from forming on cubes.

2 cups thinly sliced well-ripened strawberries, washed, blotted dry, and hulled before slicing

¾ cup water

⅓ cup superfine sugar (see Note)

1½ tablespoons strained fresh lemon juice

4 large unblemished strawberries, for garnish

4 short sprigs fresh mint, for garnish

1. Put strawberries and water in food processor. Run machine non-stop until strawberries are puréed, about 30 seconds. Transfer to a 1-quart glass measuring cup. Add sugar and stir vigorously with a whisk until sugar is dissolved into mixture, about 20 seconds. Whisk in lemon juice. Pour into 2 plastic 16-cube ice cube trays and freeze until firm, about 4 hours.

2. When ready to serve, pop one tray of frozen cubes into a low wide bowl. (If you have difficulty removing frozen cubes, run bottom of tray briefly under tepid water to loosen.) Place in food processor and process by pulsing 10 to 12 times with quick on/off action until no large chunks of ice remain and texture is smooth. Spoon into two 8-ounce wine goblets. Repeat with remaining cubes. Garnish with fresh strawberries and mint; serve immediately.

Note: Superfine sugar can be made in food processor. Place ⅓ cup granulated sugar in food processor and run machine nonstop for 30 seconds until texture is superfine.

Per Serving: Cal. 90   Carb. 23 gm   Chol. 0 mg
             Fat .30 gm   Prot. 1 gm   Sod. 1 mg

Walnut and Orange Cake

[Torta di Noci ed Aranci]

14 SLICES

To cut back on the calories and fat in this cake, the shortening has been replaced with applesauce. This moist Sicilian cake can be made one day before serving. Cover with plastic wrap and store in cool place until ready to use.

1¾ cups unbleached all-purpose flour
2 teaspoons baking powder
1 teaspoon ground cinnamon
⅔ cup walnuts
1 large whole egg at room temperature
3 large egg whites, at room temperature
¾ cup sugar
1 tablespoon grated zest from navel orange

½ cup strained fresh orange juice
2 teaspoons pure vanilla extract
⅓ cup unsweetened applesauce
1 tablespoon sifted confectioners' sugar, for garnish

1. Adjust oven rack one-third up from bottom of oven and preheat to 350°F. Lightly grease a round 10 × 2-inch cake pan with olive oil cooking spray and dust with flour; set aside.
2. Put flour, baking powder, cinnamon, and walnuts in food processor. Process until nuts are finely ground, about 20 seconds; set aside.
3. In bowl of electric mixer, beat whole egg and egg whites on medium-high speed until light in color, about 4 minutes. Gradually add sugar and continue beating until mixture is thick and glossy, about 5 minutes.

4. Add orange zest, juice, vanilla extract, and applesauce. Turn machine to low and beat until blended, about 10 seconds. Add all the flour-nut mixture and beat on low speed just until incorporated, about 20 seconds. Pour batter into prepared pan and tap gently to dislodge air bubbles. Center the pan on rack and bake in preheated oven until cake is lightly golden and cake tester inserted in center comes out clean, about 30 to 35 minutes. Let cake cool in pan on wire rack for 15 minutes. Invert onto rack, remove pan, and invert again onto second rack. Let cake cool completely before transferring to cake plate. Dust with confectioners' sugar just before serving.

Per Serving: Cal. 143   Carb. 25 mg   Chol. 15 mg
               Fat 3 gm   Prot. 3 gm   Sod. 87 mg

Cookies

[Biscotti]

It seems that these traditional crunchy cookies or biscotti have become the rage with Americans. They can be found everywhere today: in handsome packages at supermarkets or specialty food stores, on restaurant menus, and at the numerous coffee houses springing up all over the country, where they are natural companions to either espresso or cappuccino. They can stand on their own as dessert or provide a perfect accompaniment to any of the fruit or granita recipes in the dessert chapter. While there are many varieties of biscotti, they all have one thing in common. As the name suggests, biscotti are twice-baked. (In Italian, "bis" means twice and "cotti" translates to baked.)

I vividly remember my father-in-law, Vincenzo Casale, who was an Italian pastry chef of the first order, telling me about his four-week ocean voyage to this country. At that time he was a pastry apprentice at the tender age of twelve. He was so excited about coming to this country, he made several different types of biscotti in advance because he knew they would keep for his long journey. His mother sewed muslin sacks, where he put his assortment of crisp cookies for sustenance. He told me how he shared his goodies with fellow passengers and even managed to get a single upper berth from a sailor by basic-biscotti-bribing. Many of the following recipes are adaptations of Papa Casale's traditional recipes. The amounts of sugar and nuts have been lowered to reduce calories and fat. Others are contemporary versions I have developed for the taste of today with less than one gram of fat in each biscuit. By incorporating unusual dried fruits and uncommon spices and flavorings I have created cookies that can be found nowhere in Italy, but are sure to find a permanent place in your heart.

Anise-Flavored Biscotti

[Biscotti d'Anice]

❖

MAKES 4½ DOZEN COOKIES

These classic, anise-flavored biscuits have been the family favorite for years. This adaptation came from my aunt, Gloria Oliva, who makes them year-round.

3 cups cake flour	¾ cup sugar
1 tablespoon double-acting baking powder	2 teaspoons pure anise extract
3 large eggs, at room temperature	1 teaspoon crushed anise seed
	1 egg white, lightly beaten

1. Adjust oven rack to center of oven and preheat to 350°F. Line a 14 × 17-inch cookie sheet with parchment paper; set aside.
2. Sift flour and baking powder into a medium bowl; set aside. Place eggs and sugar in bowl of electric mixer. Beat on high speed until thick and lemony, about 4 minutes. Stop machine and scrape inside bowl with rubber spatula. Add anise extract and anise seed; beat on low speed until blended, about 10 seconds. Add dry ingredients and beat on low speed until incorporated, about 20 seconds. Turn dough onto a lightly floured work surface (dough will be slightly sticky). With lightly floured hands, gently knead 2 to 3 times until dough begins to hold together in a smooth satiny mass; divide dough in half. Shape into 2 ropes, each approximately 10 inches long. Place ropes 3 inches apart on lined pan. With fingertips, lightly flatten each into a log ½ inch high, 3 inches wide, and 13 inches long. Brush logs with lightly beaten egg white.
3. Bake in preheated oven until logs are a light golden color and firm to the touch, about 20 minutes. Place cookie sheet on wire rack and cool for 8 minutes. Lower oven temperature to 325°F. Transfer logs

to cutting board. Leave parchment on baking sheet. With a serrated knife, cut logs crosswise at a slight diagonal into ½-inch-thick slices. Place half of the slices cut side down on pan, spacing them ½ inch apart. Return pan to oven and bake until dry to the touch, about 5 minutes on each side. Transfer biscotti to wire rack and cool completely. Reline pan with fresh parchment paper and repeat with remaining slices. Biscotti can be stored in a tin lined with wax paper for 3 to 4 weeks.

Per Cookie: Cal. 33   Carb. 9 gm   Chol. 13 mg
               Fat .31 gm   Prot. 1 gm   Sod. 26 mg

Blueberry Biscotti

[Biscotti di Martilli]

MAKES 5½ DOZEN COOKIES

Dried blueberries may be purchased in specialty and health food stores. If they are unavailable, 1 cup of diced (¼-inch dice) prunes may be substituted.

2½ cups unbleached all-purpose flour

⅔ cup sugar

1 teaspoon baking soda

1 teaspoon ground cinnamon

2 large eggs, at room temperature

2 large egg whites, at room temperature

1 tablespoon grated lemon zest

2 teaspoons pure vanilla extract

1 cup dried blueberries

1 large egg white, lightly beaten

1. Adjust oven rack to center of oven; preheat to 350°F. Line a 14 × 17-inch cookie sheet with parchment paper; set aside.
2. Put flour, sugar, baking soda, and cinnamon in bowl of electric mixer. Run machine on low speed to combine, about 30 seconds.
3. In a small bowl, whisk together whole eggs, 2 egg whites, lemon zest, and vanilla extract. Add to flour mixture and beat on low speed until dough starts to come together in a crumbly mass, about 30 seconds. Stir in dried blueberries. Turn dough onto a lightly floured work surface (dough will be slightly sticky). With lightly floured hands, gently knead several times until dough begins to hold together in a satiny mass; divide dough into thirds. Shape into 3 ropes approximately 11 inches long. Place ropes 2½ inches apart on lined pan. With fingertips, lightly flatten each into a log ½ inch high, 2 inches wide, and 13 inches long. Brush logs with lightly beaten egg white.
4. Bake in preheated oven until logs are golden and firm to the touch, about 25 minutes. Place cookie sheet on wire rack and cool for 8 minutes. Lower oven temperature to 325°F. Transfer logs to cutting board. Leave parchment on baking sheet. With a serrated knife, cut logs crosswise at a slight diagonal into ½-inch-thick slices. Place half of the slices cut side down on pan, spacing them ½ inch apart. Return pan to oven and bake until surfaces are lightly toasted, about 7 minutes on each side. Transfer biscotti to wire rack and cool completely. Reline pan with fresh parchment and repeat with remaining slices. Biscotti can be stored in a tin lined with wax paper for 3 weeks.

Per Cookie: Cal. 38   Carb. 8 mg   Chol. 6 mg
             Fat .19 gm   Prot. 1 gm   Sod. 24 mg

Cherry-Walnut Biscotti

[Biscotti di Ciliegie e Noce]

❖

MAKES 6 DOZEN COOKIES

Tart dried cherries may be purchased at gourmet and health food stores. If they are unavailable, coarsely chopped dark raisins may be substituted.

¾ cup walnuts
2½ cups unbleached all-purpose flour
¾ cup sugar
1½ teaspoons double-acting baking powder
½ teaspoon baking soda
2 large eggs, at room temperature

2 large egg whites, at room temperature
1 tablespoon grated zest of navel orange
2 teaspoons pure vanilla extract
1 cup coarsely chopped dried tart cherries
1 egg white, lightly beaten

1. Adjust oven rack to center of oven; preheat to 350°F. Place walnuts on small cookie sheet and toast until lightly golden, about 7 minutes. Transfer walnuts to a cutting board, cool slightly, chop fine, and set aside. Leave oven on.
2. Line a 14 × 17-inch cookie sheet with parchment paper; set aside.
3. Place flour, sugar, baking powder, and baking soda in bowl of electric mixer. Run machine on low speed to combine, about 30 seconds.
4. In a small bowl, whisk together whole eggs, 2 egg whites, orange zest, and vanilla extract. Add to flour mixture and beat on low speed until dough starts to come together in a crumbly mass, about 30 seconds. Stir in dried cherries and walnuts. Turn dough onto a well-floured work surface (dough will be soft and sticky). With well-floured hands, gently knead several times until dough begins to hold together in a sticky mass; divide dough into thirds. Shape

into 3 ropes, each approximately 12 inches long. Place ropes 2½ inches apart on the lined pan. With fingertips, lightly flatten each into a log ½ inch high, 2½ inches wide, and 14 inches long. Brush logs with lightly beaten egg white.

5. Bake in preheated oven until logs are a deep golden color and firm to the touch, about 25 minutes. Place cookie sheet on wire rack and cool for 7 minutes. Lower oven temperature to 325°F. Transfer logs to cutting board. Leave parchment on baking sheet. With a serrated knife, cut logs crosswise at a slight diagonal into ½-inch-thick slices. Place half of the slices cut side down on pan, spacing them ½ inch apart. Return pan to oven and bake until surfaces are lightly toasted, about 8 minutes on each side. Transfer biscotti to wire rack and cool completely. Reline pan with fresh parchment and repeat with remaining slices. Biscotti can be stored in a tin lined with wax paper for 3 weeks.

Per Cookie: Cal. 37   Carb. 8 gm   Chol. 6 mg
                   Fat .75 gm   Prot. 1 gm   Sod. 25 mg

Cranberry-Pistachio Biscotti

[Biscotti alla Anna]

MAKES 7 DOZEN COOKIES

Friends and family always request these biscotti for Thanksgiving. Dried cranberries are available at specialty food stores and some supermarkets, especially during the fall season. Be sure to purchase enough so that you can use some and freeze some. They can be kept frozen up to 6 months in Ziploc bags.

1 cup shelled natural pistachio nuts

1 cup dried cranberries

2½ cups unbleached all-purpose flour

1 cup sugar

1 teaspoon baking soda

¼ teaspoon salt

2 large eggs, at room temperature

2 large egg whites, at room temperature

1 tablespoon grated zest of navel orange

2 teaspoons pure vanilla extract

1 large egg white, lightly beaten

1. Adjust oven rack to center of oven; preheat to 350°F. Place pistachio nuts on a small cookie sheet and toast until lightly golden, about 7 minutes. Cool to room temperature and set aside. Leave oven on.

2. In a small bowl, combine cranberries with enough hot water to cover and let them soak for 5 minutes. Drain cranberries, blot dry with paper towel, and set aside.

3. Line a 14 × 17-inch cookie sheet with parchment paper; set aside.

4. Place flour, sugar, baking soda, and salt in bowl of electric mixer. Run machine on low speed to combine, about 30 seconds.

5. In a small bowl, whisk together whole eggs, 2 egg whites, orange zest, and vanilla extract. Add to flour mixture and beat on low speed until dough starts to come together in a crumbly mass, about 30 seconds. Stir in cranberries and pistachios. Turn dough onto a well-floured work surface (dough will be soft and sticky). With well-floured hands, gently knead several times until dough holds together in a slightly sticky mass; divide into thirds. Shape into 3 ropes, each approximately 13 inches long. Place ropes 2½ inches apart on lined pan. With fingertips, lightly flatten each into a log ½ inch high, 2½ inches wide, and 15 inches long. Brush logs with lightly beaten egg white.

6. Bake in preheated oven until logs are a deep golden color and firm to the touch, about 25 minutes. Place cookie sheet on wire rack and cool for 8 minutes. Lower oven temperature to 325°F. Transfer logs to cutting board. Leave parchment on baking sheet. With a serrated knife, cut logs crosswise on a slight diagonal into ½-inch-thick slices.

Place half of the slices cut side down on pan, spacing them ½ inch apart. Return pan to oven and bake until surfaces are lightly toasted, about 8 minutes on each side. Transfer biscotti to wire rack and cool completely. Reline pan with fresh parchment paper and repeat with remaining slices. Biscotti can be stored in a tin lined with wax paper for 3 weeks.

Per Cookie: Cal. 34   Carb. 6 gm   Chol. 5 mg

                 Fat .87 gm   Prot. 1 gm   Sod. 25 mg

Chocolate-Almond Biscotti

[Biscotti alla Vincenzo]

MAKES 5 DOZEN COOKIES

These biscotti make great holiday or hostess gifts for chocolate lovers. The Dutch-process cocoa and toasted almonds contribute a double flavor impact to this enticing variation.

¾ cup natural whole almonds	2 large eggs, at room temperature
2 cups unbleached all-purpose flour	2 large egg whites, at room temperature
¾ cup sugar	1½ teaspoons pure vanilla extract
⅓ cup unsweetened Dutch-process cocoa	1 egg white, lightly beaten
2 teaspoons instant espresso coffee powder	
2 teaspoons double-acting baking powder	

1. Adjust oven rack to center of oven; preheat to 350°F. Place almonds on small cookie sheet and toast until the skins are a deep

golden color, about 9 minutes. Transfer to a cutting board, cool slightly, chop coarsely, and set aside. Leave oven on.

2. Line a 14 × 17-inch cookie sheet with parchment paper; set aside.

3. Place flour, sugar, cocoa, coffee powder, and baking powder in bowl of electric mixer. Run machine on low speed to combine, about 40 seconds.

4. In a small bowl, whisk together whole eggs, 2 egg whites, and vanilla extract. Add to flour mixture and beat on low speed until dough starts to come together in a crumbly mass, about 30 seconds. Stir in almonds. Turn dough onto a well-floured work surface (dough will be soft and sticky). With well-floured hands, gently knead 2 to 3 times until dough begins to hold together in a sticky mass; divide dough into thirds. Shape into 3 ropes, each approximately 11 inches long. Place ropes 3 inches apart on lined pan. With fingertips, lightly flatten each into a log ½ inch high, 2½ inches wide, and 13 inches long. Brush logs with lightly beaten egg white.

5. Bake in preheated oven until logs are firm to the touch, about 20 minutes. Place cookie sheet on wire rack and cool for 5 minutes. Lower oven temperature to 325°F. Transfer logs to cutting board. Leave parchment on baking sheet. With a serrated knife, cut logs crosswise at a slight diagonal into ½-inch-thick slices. Place half of the slices cut side down on pan, spacing them ½ inch apart. Return to oven and bake until surfaces are dry to the touch, about 7 minutes on each side. Transfer biscotti to wire rack and cool completely. Reline pan with fresh parchment and repeat with remaining slices. Biscotti can be stored in a tin lined with wax paper for 3 weeks.

Per Cookie:	Cal. 40	Carb. 7 gm	Chol. 8 mg
	Fat .90	Prot. 1 gm	Sod. 27 mg

Espresso-Hazelnut Biscotti

[Biscotti di Nocciuola con Espresso]

❖

MAKES 5 DOZEN COOKIES

These crispy cookies are wonderful when paired with a coffee beverage such as cappuccino or caffe latte. If hazelnuts are unavailable, you may substitute filberts. Follow same procedure for toasting.

¾ cup hazelnuts
2 tablespoons plus 1 teaspoon instant espresso coffee powder
2½ tablespoons coffee liqueur, preferably Kahlúa
2½ cups unbleached all-purpose flour
¾ cup sugar
2 teaspoons double-acting baking powder

2 large eggs, at room temperature
2 large egg whites, at room temperature
2 teaspoons pure vanilla extract
1 large egg white, lightly beaten

1. Adjust oven rack to center of oven; preheat to 350°F. Place hazelnuts on small cookie sheet and toast until nuts are a dark golden color and skins blister, about 10 minutes. Place nuts in a dish towel and rub to remove skins. Transfer to a cutting board, cool slightly, chop coarsely, and set aside. Leave oven on.
2. In a small ovenproof bowl, combine coffee powder and coffee liqueur. Place on bottom rack in oven (while nuts are toasting) for 5 minutes to steep. (Alternatively, combine in a microwave-safe bowl and microwave on HIGH for 20 seconds to steep.) Set aside and cool to room temperature.
3. Line a 14 × 17-inch cookie sheet with parchment paper; set aside.

4. Place flour, sugar, and baking powder in bowl of electric mixer. Run machine on low speed to combine, about 40 seconds.

5. In a small bowl, whisk together whole eggs, 2 egg whites, coffee mixture, and vanilla. Add to flour mixture and beat on low speed until dough starts to come together in a crumbly mass, about 30 seconds. Stir in hazelnuts. Turn dough onto a well-floured work surface (dough will be soft and sticky). With lightly floured hands, gently knead several times until dough begins to hold together in a slightly sticky mass; divide dough into thirds. Shape into 3 ropes approximately 12 inches long. Place ropes 3 inches apart on lined pan. With fingertips, lightly flatten each into a log ½ inch high, 2½ inches wide, and 14 inches long. Brush logs with lightly beaten egg white.

6. Bake in preheated oven until logs are a deep golden color and firm to the touch, about 20 minutes. Place cookie sheet on wire rack and cool for 8 minutes. Lower oven temperature to 325°F. Transfer logs to cutting board. Leave parchment on baking sheet. With a serrated knife, cut logs crosswise on a slight diagonal into ½-inch-thick slices. Place half of the slices cut side down on pan, spacing them ½ inch apart. Return to oven and bake until surfaces are lightly toasted, about 7 minutes on each side. Transfer biscotti to wire rack and cool completely. Reline pan with fresh parchment and repeat with remaining slices. Biscotti can be stored in a tin lined with wax paper for 3 weeks.

Per Cookie: Cal. 38   Carb. 6 gm   Chol. 7 mg
               Fat .80 gm   Prot. 1 gm   Sod. 21 mg

Lemon-Walnut Biscotti

[Biscotti alla Anna]

MAKES 6 DOZEN COOKIES

The slight hint of black pepper combined with lemon zest adds zippy flavor to these twice-baked biscuits.

1 cup walnuts	2 large eggs, at room temperature
2½ cups unbleached all-purpose flour	2 large egg whites, at room temperature
¾ cup sugar	4 teaspoons grated lemon zest
2 teaspoons double-acting baking powder	1 teaspoon pure lemon extract
¼ teaspoon salt	1 large egg white, lightly beaten
1 teaspoon finely milled black pepper	

1. Adjust oven rack to center of oven; preheat to 350°F. Place walnuts on small cookie sheet and toast until lightly golden, about 7 minutes. Transfer walnuts to a cutting board, cool slightly, chop coarsely, and set aside. Leave oven on.
2. Line a 14 × 7-inch cookie sheet with parchment paper; set aside.
3. Place flour, sugar, baking powder, salt, and pepper in bowl of electric mixer. Run machine on low speed to combine, about 30 seconds.
4. In a small bowl, whisk together whole eggs, 2 egg whites, lemon zest, and lemon extract. Add to flour mixture and beat on low speed until dough starts to come together in a crumbly mass, about 30 seconds. Stir in walnuts. Turn dough onto a lightly floured work surface (dough will be soft and slightly sticky). With lightly floured

hands, gently knead several times until dough holds together; divide into thirds. Shape into 3 ropes each approximately 13 inches long. Place ropes 2½ inches apart on lined pan. With fingertips, lightly flatten each into a log ½ inch high, 2½ inches wide, and 15 inches long. Brush logs with lightly beaten egg white.

5. Bake in preheated oven until logs are lightly golden and firm to the touch, about 25 minutes. Place cookie sheet on wire rack and cool for 5 minutes. Lower oven temperature to 325°F. Transfer logs to cutting board. Leave parchment on baking sheet. With a serrated knife, cut logs crosswise at a slight diagonal into ½-inch-thick slices. Place half of the slices cut side down on pan, spacing them ½ inch apart. Return pan to oven and bake until surfaces are dry to the touch, about 6 minutes on each side. Transfer biscotti to wire rack and cool completely. Reline pan with fresh parchment paper and repeat with remaining slices. Biscotti can be stored in a tin lined with wax paper for 3 weeks.

Per Cookie: Cal. 33   Carb. 6 gm   Chol. 6 mg
              Fat .80 gm   Prot. 1 gm   Sod. 25 mg

Mochaccino Biscotti

[Biscotti Mochaccino]

MAKES 6½ DOZEN COOKIES

The subtle blending of coffee, cocoa, and cinnamon linger long after the last bite of these delicate, crispy cookies, delicious dunking partners with a cup of coffee, cocoa, or a glass of cold milk.

〜〜

3½ cups cake flour

1 tablespoon double-acting baking powder

2 tablespoons instant espresso coffee powder

2 tablespoons Dutch-process cocoa

1 teaspoon ground cinnamon

2 large eggs, at room temperature

2 large egg whites, at room temperature

¾ cup sugar

2 teaspoons pure vanilla extract

1 large egg white, lightly beaten

1. Adjust oven rack to center of oven and preheat to 350°F. Line a 14 × 17-inch cookie sheet with parchment paper; set aside.

2. Sift flour, baking powder, coffee powder, cocoa, and cinnamon into a medium bowl.

3. Place whole eggs, 2 egg whites, and sugar in bowl of electric mixer. Beat on high speed until thick and lemony, about 4 minutes. Stop machine and scrape down bowl with rubber spatula. Add vanilla extract and beat on low speed until blended, about 10 seconds. Add dry ingredients and beat on low speed until incorporated, about 30 seconds. Turn dough onto a lightly floured work surface (dough will be slightly sticky). With lightly floured hands, gently knead 2 to 3 times until dough begins to hold together in a smooth satiny mass; divide dough into thirds. Shape into 3 ropes, each approximately 11 inches long. Place ropes 3 inches apart on lined pan. With fingertips, lightly flatten each into a log ½ inch high, 2 inches wide, and 13 inches long. Brush logs with lightly beaten egg white.

4. Bake in preheated oven until logs are firm to the touch, about 18 minutes. Place cookie sheet on wire rack and cool for 5 minutes. Lower oven temperature to 300°F. Transfer logs to cutting board. Leave parchment on baking sheet. With a serrated knife, cut logs crosswise at a slight diagonal into ½-inch-thick slices. Place half of the slices cut side down on pan, spacing them ½ inch apart. Return pan to oven and bake until dry to the touch, about 6 minutes on each side. Transfer biscotti to wire rack and cool completely. Reline pan with fresh parchment paper and repeat with remaining slices. Biscotti can be stored in a tin lined with wax paper for 3 to 4 weeks.

Per Cookie:	Cal. 29	Carb. 6 gm	Chol. 5 mg
	Fat .18 gm	Prot. 1 gm	Sod. 24 mg

Orange-Almond Biscotti

[Biscotti alla Toscana]

MAKES 6 DOZEN COOKIES

These classic Italian dunking biscotti are traditional to the region of Tuscany where they are usually served with Vin Santo, a sweet dessert wine. They are also a perfect accompaniment to a cup of espresso or cappuccino.

- ¾ cup natural whole almonds
- 2 cups unbleached all-purpose flour
- ¾ cup sugar
- 2 teaspoons double-acting baking powder
- ⅛ teaspoon salt
- 2 large eggs, at room temperature
- 2 large egg whites, at room temperature
- 4 teaspoons grated zest of navel orange
- 2 teaspoons pure vanilla extract
- 1 large egg white, lightly beaten

1. Adjust oven rack to center of oven and preheat to 350°F. Place almonds on small cookie sheet and toast until the skins are a deep golden color, about 9 minutes. Transfer to a cutting board, cool slightly, chop coarsely, and set aside. Leave oven on.
2. Line a 14 × 17-inch cookie sheet with parchment paper; set aside.
3. Place flour, sugar, baking powder, and salt in bowl of electric mixer. Run machine on low speed to combine, about 30 seconds.
4. In a small bowl, whisk together whole eggs, 2 egg whites, orange zest, and vanilla extract. Add to flour mixture and beat on low

speed until dough starts to come together in a crumbly mass, about 30 seconds. Stir in almonds. Turn dough onto a lightly floured work surface (dough will be soft and slightly sticky). With lightly floured hands, gently knead several times until dough holds together; divide into thirds. Shape into 3 ropes, each approximately 11 inches long. Place ropes 2½ inches apart on lined pan. With fingertips, lightly flatten each into a log ½ inch high, 2½ inches wide, and 14 inches long. Brush logs with lightly beaten egg white.

5. Bake in preheated oven until logs are lightly golden and firm to the touch, about 20 minutes. Place cookie sheet on wire rack and cool for 5 minutes. Lower oven temperature to 325°F. Transfer logs to cutting board. Leave parchment on baking sheet. With a serrated knife, cut logs crosswise at a slight diagonal into ½-inch-thick slices. Place half of the slices cut side down on pan, spacing them ½ inch apart. Return pan to oven and bake until surfaces are dry to the touch, about 6 minutes on each side. Transfer biscotti to wire rack and cool completely. Reline pan with fresh parchment paper and repeat with remaining slices. Biscotti can be stored in a tin lined with wax paper for 3 weeks.

Per Cookie: Cal. 32   Carb. 5 gm   Chol. 6 mg
             Fat .86 gm   Prot. 1 gm   Sod. 22 mg

Pear and Ginger Biscotti

[Biscotti di Pere e Zenzero]

MAKES 6½ DOZEN COOKIES

These unusual, spicy biscuits are totally unlike anything you will ever find in Italy. I developed this recipe for anyone who loves the flavoring of ginger.

ᏫᏫ

2½ cups unbleached all-purpose bleached flour

¾ cup well-packed light brown sugar

1¼ teaspoons baking soda

2 teaspoons ground ginger

2 large eggs, at room temperature

2 large egg whites, at room temperature

2 teaspoons pure vanilla extract

1 cup dried pear halves, preferably Bartletts (about 5 ounces), cut into ¼-inch dice

¼ cup minced crystallized ginger

1 large egg white, lightly beaten

1. Adjust oven rack to center of oven and preheat to 350°F. Line a 14 × 17-inch cookie sheet with parchment paper; set aside.

2. Place flour, brown sugar, baking soda, and ground ginger in bowl of electric mixer. Run machine on low speed to combine, about 30 seconds.

3. In a small bowl, whisk together whole eggs, 2 egg whites, and vanilla extract. Add to flour mixture and beat on low speed until dough starts to come together in a crumbly mass, about 30 seconds. Stir in pears and crystallized ginger. Turn dough onto a well-floured work surface (dough will be soft and sticky). With lightly floured hands, gently knead several times until dough holds together in a slightly sticky mass; divide dough into thirds. Shape into 3 ropes, each approximately 12 inches long. Place ropes 2½ inches apart on lined pan. With fingertips, lightly flatten each into a log ½ inch high, 2 inches wide, and 14 inches long. Brush logs with lightly beaten egg white.

4. Bake in preheated oven until logs are a deep golden color and firm to the touch, about 20 minutes. Place cookie sheet on wire rack and cool for 9 minutes. Lower oven temperature to 325°F. Transfer logs to cutting board. Leave parchment on baking sheet. With a serrated knife, cut logs crosswise at a slight diagonal into ½-inch-thick slices. Place half of the slices cut side down on pan, spacing them ½ inch apart. Return pan to oven and bake until surfaces are light toasted, about 8 minutes on each side. Transfer biscotti to wire rack and cool completely. Reline pan with fresh parchment and repeat with remaining slices. Biscotti can be stored in tin lined with wax paper for 3 weeks.

Per Cookie: Cal. 31   Carb. 8 mg   Chol. 6 mg
               Fat .17 gm   Prot. 1 gm   Sod. 26 mg

Whole-Wheat and Apricot Biscotti

[Biscotti alla Giovanni]

MAKES 6½ DOZEN COOKIES

These are my husband John's favorite dunking biscotti. The macerated dried apricots lend a chewy bite to these crunchy cookies.

1 cup well-packed dried apricots, cut into ¼-inch dice	1 teaspoon ground cinnamon
¼ cup Cognac or brandy	2 large eggs, at room temperature
1 cup whole-wheat flour	2 large egg whites, at room temperature
1¾ cups unbleached all-purpose flour	1½ teaspoons pure almond extract
⅔ cup sugar	1 egg white, lightly beaten
1 teaspoon baking soda	
1 teaspoon double-acting baking powder	

1. Place apricots in a small bowl; stir in Cognac, cover with plastic wrap, and set aside to macerate for 15 minutes.
2. Adjust oven rack to center of oven and preheat to 350°F. Line a 14 × 17-inch cookie sheet with parchment paper; set aside.
3. Place whole-wheat flour, all-purpose flour, sugar, baking soda, baking powder, and cinnamon in bowl of electric mixer. Run machine on low speed to combine, about 40 seconds.

4. In a small bowl, whisk together whole eggs, 2 egg whites, and almond extract. Add to flour mixture and beat on low speed until dough starts to come together in a crumbly mass, about 30 seconds. Stir in macerated fruit. Turn dough onto a well-floured work surface (dough will be very soft and sticky). With well-floured hands, gently knead several times until dough holds together in a slightly sticky mass; divide dough into thirds. Shape into 3 ropes, each approximately 11 inches long. Place ropes 2½ inches apart on lined pan. With fingertips, lightly flatten each into a log ½ inch high, 2½ inches wide, and 13 inches long. Brush logs with lightly beaten egg white.

5. Bake in preheated oven until logs are a deep golden color and firm to the touch, about 20 minutes. Place cookie sheet on wire rack and cool for 7 minutes. Transfer logs to cutting board. Leave parchment on baking sheet. With a serrated knife, cut logs crosswise at a slight diagonal into ½-inch slices. Place half of the slices cut side down on pan, spacing them ½ inch apart. Return pan to oven and bake until lightly toasted, about 10 minutes on each side. Transfer biscotti to wire rack and cool completely. Reline pan with fresh parchment paper and repeat with remaining slices. Biscotti can be stored in a tin lined with wax paper for 3 to 4 weeks.

Per Cookie:	Cal. 30	Carb. 6 gm	Chol. 5 mg
	Fat .16 gm	Prot. 1 gm	Sod. 26 mg

Index

~~~~~~

〰〰〰〰〰〰〰〰〰〰〰〰〰〰〰〰〰〰〰〰〰〰〰〰〰〰〰〰〰〰〰〰〰〰〰〰〰〰〰

ABOUT THE AUTHOR

ANNE CASALE began teaching cooking in 1963 when she founded Annie's Kitchen. She served as president of The New York Association of Cooking Teachers for two terms. She is also a Certified Culinary Professional of the International Association of Culinary Professionals. She has taught in cooking schools throughout the United States and has appeared on numerous television and radio programs. Ms. Casale has worked in sales and marketing and as a lecturer, consultant, and designer for restaurants, gourmet shops, and cooking schools. Ms. Casale is the author of *Italian Family Cooking, The Long Life Cookbook*, and *Lean Italian Cooking*.